Hell Here

Helen Astin-Hardman

Hell Here

First published in Great Britain in 2024
by: LOTUS BOOKS
An imprint of PARTNERSHIP PUBLISHING

Written By Helen Astin-Hardman

The editors have ensured a true reflection of the author's tone and voice has remained present throughout.

A CIP catalogue record for this book is available from the British Library.
ISBN 978-1-915200-78-5

Book Cover Design by: Partnership Publishing
Book Type Set by: Partnership Publishing

Book Published by:
PARTNERSHIP PUBLISHING
Lincolnshire, United Kingdom
www.partnershippublishing.co.uk

Printed in England.

Partnership Publishing is committed to a sustainable future for our business, our readers and our planet. This book is made from paper certified by the Forestry Stewardship Council (FSC), an organisation dedicated to promoting responsible management of forest resources.

Hell Here

To Ella Rule thankyou
for the support Comrade.
Helen A-H

Helen Astin-Hardman

Dedicated to all those unable to recover from schizophrenia.

And to Rob.

Acknowledgements

Thank you to Lynn Reynolds, a very good friend, who was the first person removed from my situation, and the absurdity of it, to whom I dared show this book.

Thank you for your kind words and encouragement.

About the book

This book details the story of my descent into paranoid schizophrenia, or psychosis as some people prefer to term it these days.

In this narrative I use the older medical term paranoid schizophrenia, though I do occasionally use the term psychosis where I feel it is more appropriate. I use the older term because I think the word psychosis is no less misleading than the word schizophrenia. Psychosis can be a symptom of many different illnesses, such as bipolar disorder, post-traumatic stress syndrome, and of course schizophrenia. I use the older name because, as I see it, changing the names of stigmatised illnesses doesn't fix the problem. It's attitudes that need to change, not words.

It is important to note that the illness that is paranoid schizophrenia should not be mistaken for split personality disorder, now named dissociative identity disorder. Although I heard several different voices in my head, I did not have different personalities.

This book is written as a series of letters to people who were there throughout my life and my illness. Some of the letters take on an apologetic tone, whereas others are purely to let the audience know what I was thinking and feeling at the time.

These were not letters I wrote during the course of my illness, and the dates on them serve to clarify the time period each letter is dealing with. I've made these dates as accurate as I can recall, though this involved some guess work. As you will see schizophrenia does confuse the mind.

Some of the letters are reminiscences, telling parts of the story the addressee would already know, but this is just so the reader can better grasp what happened to me whilst ill.

The letters to the voices in my head tell parts of the story that no physical person could see happening, because it was the voices alone who were present during these moments.

In this book I do not physically describe most of the people I encounter. This is because my story is real, and so are the people within it. There is a lot that is taboo in it, and I would prefer the people I mention not to be readily identifiable.

Finally, this story is a very personal one. There are aspects of it that some people may find comical. But let me be clear, my experience of mental illness was in no way amusing: it was torture.

Preface

A lot has changed since I first wrote this book, which I originally wrote between 2020-2022.

One of the major changes in my life came when I realised I no longer considered myself or my beliefs to come under the banner of Satanism. As I slowly became more politically aware, I decided calling my beliefs Satanism really no longer fit.

I joined the CPGB-ML in 2023, a communist party, it took me a while to come to the conclusion that I wanted to join them, and do work with them, I decided I could no longer sit on the sidelines and watch world events unfold around me.

LaVeyan Satanism which I based some of my beliefs upon really no longer fits, LaVey advocates getting by in the current system and doesn't champion a self sacrificing nature, believing instead that self preservation is the highest human instinct. In deciding to be a communist this outlook didn't suit me, I realise that there is more politics within Satanism than I realised, but not the sort of politics I actually agree with.

Many of my opinions around my former religion have changed and though I had a reluctance to rewrite my book a lot has changed to the point where it feels the opinions I had no longer reflect me.

The original story was very beautiful and had an over arching theme of a quest for faith, that I feel may be lost in my rewrite, though I still hold some spiritual beliefs I don't feel they can be called Satanism, The link was very tenuous in the first place. Though I did love my religion the time has come to part ways.

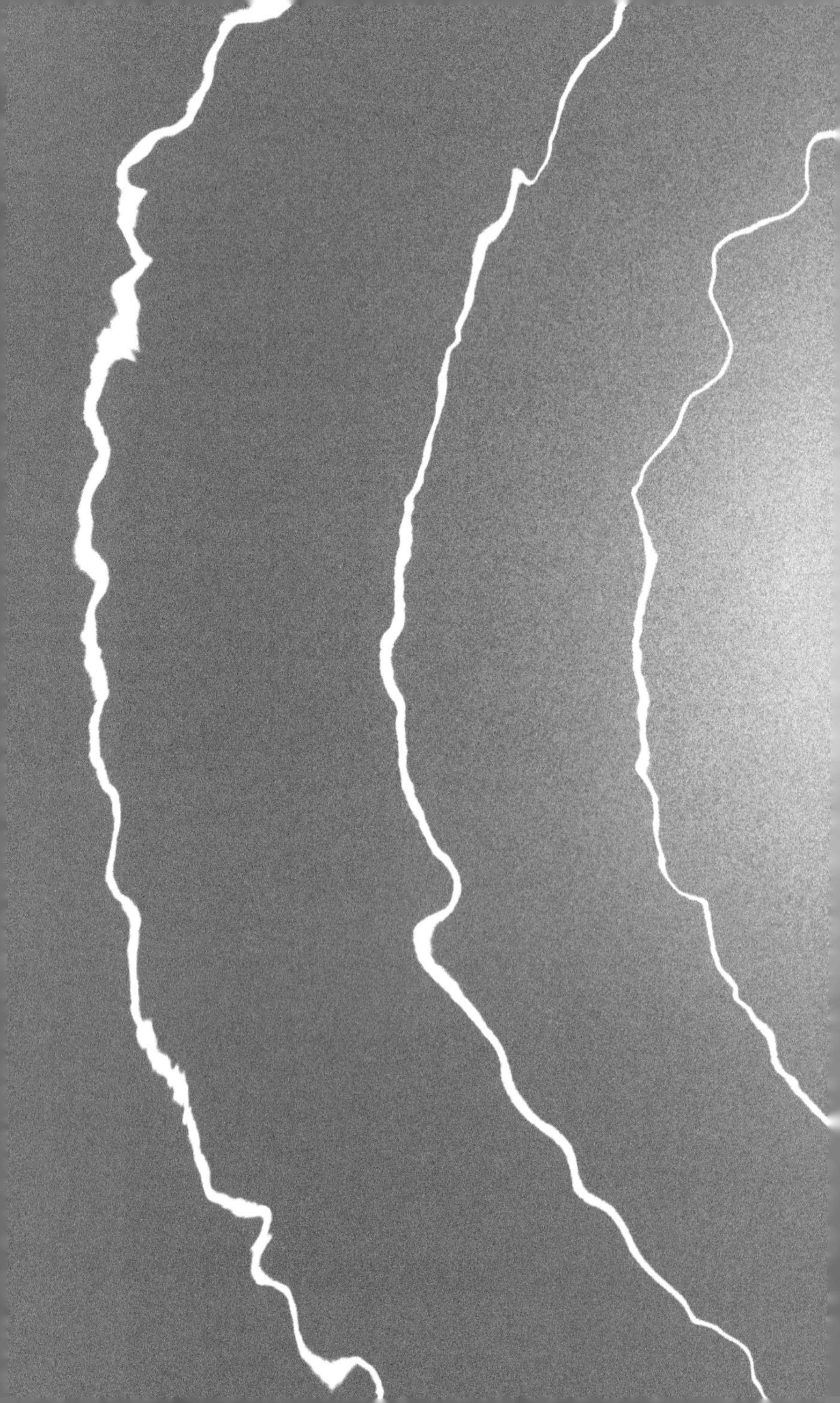

Part One

Descent

O Tortured One

O tortured one, how sweetly doth thou sing.
You look so thin, o tortured one.
Please shield the rage within.

O tortured one, hide beneath your desk.
You look so stressed, o tortured one,
what got you in this mess?

O tortured one, they thought you pretty.
But now they think you're petty.
But none of them did give you pity.

O tortured one.
O tortured one.

You always believed in me, didn't you? Despite what was going on, you always said I was a great person, I believed this too.

You'd often say I was a genius.

Many times you would seem very proud of me, and whenever I was being bullied by them, you always staunchly defended me and made me feel, however temporarily, better about myself and the situation. I never really knew much about you or your motivation for helping me to find some dignity in the tatters of what my life had become.

You were always there where I could reach you, and I looked to you to make myself feel better.

Thank you for being there, even though I don't know if I can call you a friend.

Letter to the Voices: Part One
Doncaster
The Present

Before

I heard you talking, even back then.
I felt your presence again and again.
There were no questions on my mind,
I'd always suffered hallucinations of this kind.
So I didn't think there was much wrong,
that people would naturally discuss me and harass me all along.
As sleep disappeared into the mist,
I didn't think to ask, didn't get the gist.
I was falling slowly, had been falling slowly for a very long time,
and the aftermath to me seems an uphill climb.

There you are again! If I stop and think for a second, I can hear you. Your words are often highly critical.

I have still not untangled where you came from. Did you represent my guilt over things I did, or thought I did? And why, if this were the case, did some of you occasionally say nice things about me? Or if not actually nice things, things I liked to hear?

Most people would not like to be thought of as the Antichrist, or have it said that they copulate with demons. In this regard I may have been a different person to many others. Not all, but many.

I date the beginning of my psychosis, the stage of paranoid schizophrenia which is marked by hallucinations and delusions, to around May or June 2006. Yes, it has taken me this long to come to terms with what you did to me, and what I did to myself, to be able to bear to write it down.

You, the voices, had been with me well before 2006. I just never realised it until afterwards. It was only post-medication, after the haze of delusion was stripped away, that I realised you had never been real.

Sometimes during my years in sixth form at school, around 2003- 2005, I would be in the common room and I'd hear crowds of people discussing me, only when I turned round I'd find the room mostly empty.

Often I found there was a background chatter in my head which seemed to follow me around.

And during this time I'd register only mild confusion when it turned out that the corridor which I'd been walking down was devoid of people. Schizophrenia robbed me of my sanity, so even though I could hear your voices, and see that the corridor or common room were empty of life, I couldn't put two and two together. I simply did not possess the rationality.

My years in sixth form were marked by what the medical community calls the prodromal phase, in which I wasn't yet entirely delusional, but was beginning to get extremely ill.

Nowadays you are my constant companions, because the medication doesn't quiet you entirely.

You are reading this with me as I write. We are one.

I've tried, since being diagnosed in April 2007, to write about what happened to me when I was ill, but due to the incoherent and distorted thinking that comes with the aftermath of the illness, I've found it hard to get anything cogent down in writing. This is my latest attempt.

Fortunately, as I've slowly recovered my senses, I've become better at writing again. But even as I try write this sentence I'm still burdened with your taunts.

Of course this book will not show me, or in fact you, in a good light, my torturers. Yes: that is what you became to me.

As you know well, you created a world for me in which I believed everyone was talking about me. Though believed may not be the exactly right word, because in fact I was delusional. I was convinced I was being constantly watched by you, and that you were not voices in my head but real people, talking about me, nagging me with your constant discussions, and always second guessing my behaviours and actions.

The world you created was no mere fantasy. It was my reality, one in which I had the compulsion to listen to you. My emotions would reach dizzying heights and crushing lows, painful black pits of despair, and anger and disgust so intense they manifest as hatred, a hatred I directed at the human race.

You can't know how I feel because you are just voices, but no matter how much I remind myself of this, I can't help sensing that you are aware. You always knew just what to say to crush my spirit, giving me hope before snatching it away, gleefully taking away from me everything that mattered. Who are you?

Oh Tortured one
how sweetly doth thou sing

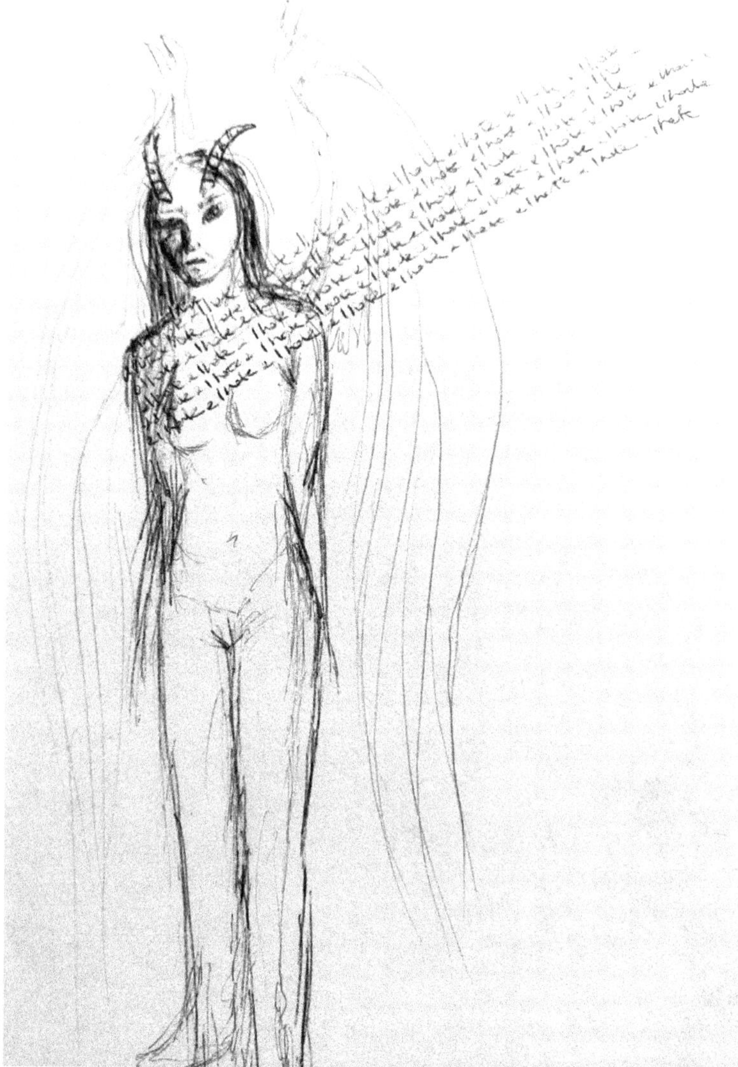

A Letter to Emma
Doncaster
2003-Present

The Fool

I lost my inhibitions the other day.
I didn't realise I'd lost them.
As all that is lost,
you notice at your cost.

I lost my ability to hope and pray.
I didn't feel they mattered anyway.
With my inhibitions went my ability to moderate,
to think clearly before I operate.

I lost my inhibitions the other day.
I never noticed where they went.
And all that is lost,
melts like winter frost.

I lost my ability to run and play.
Instead of engaging pushed people away.
Desirous of being mysterious,
tireless and ever so serious.

People they may have been curious.
But the way they laughed made me furious.
Making an image of myself.
Loss of inhibitions for reasons of health.

Emma, I write this letter to you because over the years you have been a very good friend to me, despite the fact I was not always responsive to your friendship, at least this is how I felt I behaved.

We met, I recall in the queue outside biology class, during our time in sixth form. I wish we had known each other longer, because then you might not have met me while I was getting ill, and you might have seen a side to me which hadn't been shaped by schizophrenia.

From the first time we got talking you always made loads of effort with me, even though I sometimes behaved in an aloof manner.

There were multiple reasons for my lukewarm responses to people. Most influential were the steadily darkening emotions that I now think were related to my illness. When I look back, I feel that I never made the right amount of effort with you, preferring instead to frighten the other students in the common room.

Another reason for my lack of effort was because I was steadily becoming interested in, or rather obsessed by, religion. I know now that religiosity can often be a symptom of schizophrenia. The religion I became obsessed with, however, was Satanism.

As you and possibly others may remember, I used to sit on the back of the common room sofas, hunched over my book of shadows, a black tome with a silver pentagram embossed on the cover.

I'd write in it using a quill and blood red ink. I would write out my theories and ideas in a simple cipher, one I devised to disguise what I was writing. I've always disliked making ideas permanent on a page, and feel doubly strange about my thoughts being there for all to see. There are so many pieces of paper, I've written on and later looked back and cringed, then duly thrown the paper away. This is possibly why I'm an artist at heart and not a writer.

I was extremely self-absorbed at this time in my life, I would often sit staring into space fantasising about wealth, fame, power, and supernatural prowess. I'd fantasise that I was the Antichrist, and that I'd use my powers to get back at people who were bullying me, pulling down meteors down from space and ending their lives.

If I wasn't fantasising, I'd be theorising, coming up with theological and scientific ideas about the universe, so I rarely talked, and probably appeared to outsiders to be glaring around.

My intense interest in devils and demons must have been a disturbing trait, yet you persisted with being my friend. There was little mention of my religious affiliations between us. You managed to overlook my more unsavoury elements, and accepted me for who I was.

It must have been hard going being my friend, because I spent far more time maintaining my dark image than I did caring for my peers. I very much felt that having human relationships cramped my style.

One thing we did enjoy together, and something I fully engaged with, was going to the Whitby Goth Weekend in October of each year. We both had a good time, even though I'd get internally frustrated with how slow you'd be at getting ready in the morning. But slow starts aside, I very much enjoyed going, and appreciated that you'd pick me up and drive us all the way to Whitby from Doncaster.

At the festival I loved admiring the costumes of others, and enjoyed having somewhere I could dress up in my finery. A lot of effort was put into peoples' costumes, and I found seeing how they had decided to dress up just as exciting as dressing in our own costumes.

In some ways I was not all that different to the people I labelled as ordinary, people who wouldn't be found amongst us goths.

I enjoyed shopping and adding new dimensions to my outfits, posing for the photographers up at the abbey. It's just the things I was into were seen as darker than those which other people liked.

The cobbled streets of Whitby were always heaving during the Goth Fest and we never found much room to move. I remember one occasion when you wore eight-inch heeled platform shoes, and we had to proceed really slowly so you didn't fall over on the cobbles. I was dressed in a black coat with pentagram buttons, and a demon mask I'd made, while you were dressed a stylised pirate complete with corset.

I hadn't always been as extreme in the way I chose to dress. Before I knew you I was content to wear black T-shirts, black jeans and many chains. It was an incident that happened to me in Doncaster town centre during my mid-teens which prompted me to change my style.

On that occasion I'd been with a friend shopping. We weren't shopping for anything specific, but had gone out for a leisurely browse. Me and my friend had decided to go into a gift shop and were in the process of looking at the items on display when a girl and her gang of friends spotted us. They taunted us, calling us sweaties, which was a word used for alternative people in Doncaster at the time.

We decided to leave the shop, but the gang followed singing, "Who let the dogs out?" I felt on this occasion that I looked a bit scruffy, which did heighten my sense of embarrassment during this incident. The rabble followed us up the street, and one of the girls stood in front of us barring our way. She tried to be threatening, but was younger, and a head shorter than me. She had stick-on gems on her face and was wearing a crop top, the very epitome of the sort of person who shouldn't have been commenting on anyone else's dress sense.

I confess that I felt like punching her in the face, but I restrained myself.

After that incident I resolved to dress with more dignity, so that if anyone commented or took offence I could at least feel I looked tidy.

The first long gothic coat I obtained came from Whitby. I bought it on an occasion when I went there on the back of my dad's motorcycle. The coat was made of a light floaty material, it was black of course, with fancy ruffled cuffs, and when I wore it in the wind I felt I looked dramatic.

You'll have seen me wear it a lot during my first year of sixth form, as it was an item of clothing I rarely removed. I was always thankful that our school uniform happened to be black.

People in school used to insult me because of my gothic dress sense and would mock the fact that I always wore the coat. One student was incredulous when he asked what I'd paid for it, and I replied it had cost £60. He obviously didn't appreciate this is at the cheaper end of gothic clothes.

In my second year of sixth form I acquired many different coats. One of these had been custom made for me. I owned so many coats because they were my favourite item of clothing, but also because people mocked me for always dressing the same every day. They conflated my never-changing style with poor hygiene, as if wearing the same coat amounted to not washing.

Appearing in a variety of coats meant the bullies were deprived of at least some ammunition.

During my years in sixth form I collected many props and accessories, including my articulated claw rings, and a bowler hat with netting over the face that I obtained on a school trip to London in our first year. And sometimes in flagrant violation of the uniform code, I would also carry a cane, a black slender shiny one with a pearly white orb on top.

The teachers variously helped or hindered me in my style choices. Some of the teachers would see me with claws and a cane and confiscate the items till the end of the day. Others like our biology teacher would let me get away with it. When the other students questioned his leniency, he'd give the excuse that I was technically still wearing my uniform, complete with tie, underneath my coat.

On one occasion, when I was strutting along all dressed up and the headteacher of the school saw me, he tapped his nose and winked. So all in all, the schools authority figures offered a mixed bag of responses to my dress sense.

I mentioned our school trip to London, and it was on this occasion I nearly did something particularly stupid and dangerous. I mention it here because I think it offers an insight into my experience of getting ill.

For me the prodromal phase of schizophrenia was marked by an inability to sleep, an increased interest in religion, a certain emotional flatness, and a recklessness and an inability to resist impulses. It was this recklessness that nearly put me in danger.

While on the London trip I ended up in a room on my own. All the students were supposed to be sharing, but the person I was meant to be sharing with decided to go and stay in a different room with two of her friends. I didn't mind this because I preferred to be alone, and didn't really know the girl I'd been paired up with.

During the course of the trip I discovered that my friend Stuart was staying in a room on the floor below, but one window across from mine. His room also had a balcony.

The building we were staying in was what would have been, during term time, the student accommodation for the university. It was a huge, pale grey stone building, and outside my window was a wide flat ledge.

In my mind I thought it would be a cool stunt to walk across this ledge and do a fireman's drop on to Stuart's balcony. I was really quite serious about performing this stunt. The only thing that stopped me was the thought of what would happen if he wasn't in at the time. What if I ended up stuck outside on his balcony, unable to get back?

It was fortunate that I did stop and think, because the distance to the street was a long way to fall. Even if I had succeeded I could have injured myself falling onto the balcony.

Another incident which reveals what it was like for me while getting ill took place on another school trip in the second year of sixth form. We travelled to the Isle of Arran in Scotland as part of our biology module, where we studied the local wildlife, in particular the limpets.

Studying the limpets was the dullest part of the trip, because it involved measuring the height of them and comparing this measurement to the heights of the limpets further inland. The rest of the trip was a lot of fun though, and the weather was mostly sunny throughout, despite Arran being billed as the rainiest place in Britain.

My favourite part of the trip was when we all went to the coast with trays to collect creatures from under the rocks. Another day everyone seemed to enjoy was when we trekked up the mountainous terrain. I was dreading it at first, as back then I wasn't much of a walker, let alone a prolific hill climber, but the pace wasn't too fast, the scenery was gorgeous, and I kept finding interesting bugs to look at.

The incident happened when we were ready to go back home, after a week of lessons and fieldwork. We were stood in groups near the coach. I was wearing a black top with long sleeves and an inverted cross motif. I happened to glance over at a group of lads from our class, and heard one of them say about me, "she's probably going to curse us now. I hate her!"

This was said with such venom that I felt strangely upset by it. On its own this incident would not have been significant; people were often cruel to me. Except that a few weeks later in lessons, the same boy said to me, "I think you are really brave dressing the way you do and being open about your beliefs." To which I replied in surprise "Really? I thought you hated me."

While I was ill with schizophrenia this often happened. I'd hear people speak, but I wouldn't hear what they had actually said. Instead my brain would twist their words into something else, which would make me think they were talking about me. Then this in turn would cause me to listen in and think more things were being said about me. It was the definition of a vicious cycle. But it wasn't real.

While I was away at university in Huddersfield, where I became seriously ill, you wrote me numerous letters. I was in such a bad place at the time that I never did write back to you. I had truly meant to. It was one of those jobs that I relegated to another time, and then simply forgot.

Even if I had written back, you may not have received the letter anyway. On one occasion I sent my dad a birthday card. I was getting confused at the time due to my steadily developing illness, and wrote the word "Dad" on the envelope, then couldn't for the life of me figure out what else I'd missed. It was only when he told me he'd never received the card that I realised I'd posted it without an address on. No wonder the Victorians labelled schizophrenia a form of dementia, dementia praecox was the name they had for it.

Remembering these lapses makes me feel that I was in some ways not a very good friend to you.

I hope this hasn't affected our friendship. These days I feel I'm able to be a better friend than I once was.

At least you can count this amongst the letters I've actually written to you.

A Letter to the students of Storthes Hall
Huddersfield University
Sept 2005- June 2006

The Goth

Look at her, walking around like she owns the very fibres of the earth, of the sky.
So purposeful in her walk, yet going nowhere.

The heavy tread of those boots she wears, wearing out with every step.
Clack, clack, clack, her cane on the ground, like so much a phallic object, yet she is sexless.

Keeping herself to herself, her face powdered white, like the gaunt spectre of things to come.
Enduring every insult we throw at her, with her blank passionless stare.

The words dry on my mouth as she approaches, only the utterance of "Scary Mary" escapes.

She doesn't care.
Is that the ghost of a smile on her face?

There is a subtle difference between lies and deception, even though their effects are largely the same. In my view, a lie is when a person overtly speaks an untruth, whereas deception is when they present an idea and let other peoples' minds fill in the blanks.

While I was always very poor at telling lies (I fear my face will give me away, and I can imagine a million scenarios in which I'll be caught out), I feel I was very good at deception.

"Where is this going?" you might ask. For me, fantasy was a big part of my life, and in my world of fantasy I was evil and powerful. But to confine these notions to fantasy was not enough. I wanted people in the real world to believe I was evil and powerful, so I presented myself as evil to them.

You see, though I was a Satanist, most Satanism is not evil, and Satanists do not necessarily have evil intent. My deception lay not in faking my religious affiliation, but in pretending I was evil.

This kind of deception is probably not all that uncommon. People present different faces to the world all the time, depending on how they want to be seen. The school bully, for instance, may be quiet and timid at home, but at school behaves with brashness and boldness, showing an image of power and strength in order to make their desire for power a reality.

I did not want to gain power by bullying or hurting others, so I found a way around this by capturing peoples' collective imaginations and playing on their primal fears, those fears people have of the dark, of monsters; those fears felt most acutely in moments when something doesn't seem quite right.

How did I achieve this deception? You might wonder, or you might already know. Well, I gave people what they expected to see, playing on what they already believed to be true.

The media image of the Satanist is a thoroughly reliable cliché. They are invariably portrayed as always wearing black clothing accessorised with an inverted cross, as projecting a powerful air of certainty, and—of course—as evil. So this was the image I portrayed. Don't get me wrong, it wasn't a difficult subterfuge for me to pull off, as I have always been inspired by the imagery of darkness and horror. Constructing my Satanic persona allowed me to play on my enjoyment of all things dark. In reality, most Satanists dress perfectly ordinarily.

My image became even more extreme while I was at university.

There I was unhindered by the restraints of having to behave more normally, as I had to at home, since my mum didn't know that I was a Satanist.

At university I'd started to powder my face white, with black eyeliner applied very close to my eyes to make them look smaller and more masculine. I often wore demon masks I'd created, and sometimes made fake wounds on my face. I always wore my hair straight and long, and kept its natural brown colour because I didn't want to have black hair like all the other goths. I wore long coats, an inverted cross, and walked with a cane. On occasion I also wore horns.

You all started referring to me as Scary Mary.

No one really knew anything concrete about me, despite all the speculation. Many of you probably hated me, and many were probably afraid of me. Others may have wanted to engage with me but were afraid I'd be too weird if they came and broke the ice. This was a perfectly understandable set of responses to my image, which was constructed to convey that I was affiliated with Satan, that I wanted you to stay away from me, and that I was indeed scary and not to be messed with.

All this makes me sound as if I believed I was really evil, but I didn't feel that way. I wanted people to think I was evil because if they believed I was evil, then it became easier to convince myself that I was.

Now at this point you may be wondering what it is that makes someone want to be seen as evil when most people want to be perceived as good. Firstly, it was a power thing. I'd had all power taken from me by those who bullied me, and I wanted to reclaim some of it, just not by being a bully myself. Instead I decided to captivate people with my image alone. In making myself seem predatory and dangerous I never actually needed to threaten or be cruel, you see. I used the realm of the imagination as my battleground. There I was on home territory.

Secondly, the desire to be evil stemmed from the gulf between my fantasies and my reality. In primary school once, a teacher asked the class "Do you think you are a leader or a follower?" At the time I saw myself as a leader, because I worked to my own rules and was often very much a nonconformist. However, I realise now that the answer is not that simple. Because although I'm a leader in many aspects of my life, in religion I preferred to be a follower.

This is because if you yourself invent a religion or become privy to too many of its internal workings, it loses its esoteric feel. Whereas if you follow an established religion, aspects of it remain enigmatic and shrouded in mystery. It is then much easier to connect with the truth in it.

The disparity between my reality and my fantasies stemmed from my first discovery of Satanism. The first Satanic group I discovered was Anton LaVey's Church of Satan, a modern Satanic group. In modern Satanism, Satan is not seen as a literal evil entity, but instead is used as a figurehead to represent opposites to mainstream religious thought. Satanism as a religion advocates worshipping yourself as your own deity, acknowledging and glorifying your ego. In this branch of Satanism there is no animal or human sacrifice.

I very much liked the literature and ideas behind LaVey's Satanism, but there was one problem I had with it. LaVey's branch of Satanism is atheistic. He abhorred the idea of God and Satan existing, and rejected the possibility of an afterlife, saying that we should indulge in the now and not concern ourselves with divine retribution. I, however, am more agnostic.

LaVey's atheistic motivation was the reason I never joined the Church of Satan. I was a lot more open than the church allows to the possibility that there might be more to the universe than we currently realise. Though at the time I had respect for some of what LaVey talks about in his religion, I found it didn't quite fit with the way I wanted to be perceived, There is little that can justifiably be called evil in modern Satanism. At university my desires were for devils and demons to be real—hence my need to be seen as evil, after all why would you worship a devil if you are not evil yourself?—so the church's denial of the existence of these entities caused me chagrin. As you can see, the issue is complicated. I knew full well I wasn't evil, and I respected LaVey's work, but I wanted to make my fantasy world a concrete reality.

The other problem I had with LaVey's literature is that I believe in an afterlife, this belief remains still. I guess this in some way made me closer to being what LaVey would term a Christian Satanist, a believer who occupies the flip side of the Christian religion. However, much as I liked the idea of the Christian heaven and hell, and all the stories behind the Christian mythos, I was not convinced things worked quite that way. I'd say I was never fully a LaVeyan, nor was I a Christian Satanist. I categorised myself as an agnostic Satanist, one who respected LaVey's viewpoints but also believed in the possibility a real Satan, though perhaps not in the form that Christians may think of him. However one might choose to express it, the fundamental aspect of my religious outlook was that I chose Satan regardless of who he may have turned out to be.

This was how I justified my beliefs as Satanic, I still hold many of the same spiritual beliefs, though I no longer call them Satanism any more.

I've discussed how my difficulties with committing to one belief stemmed from the gap between my actual beliefs and the way I wanted things to be. Factor in my inherently sceptical nature—I question literally everything— and you have the perfect recipe for agnosticism.

There are theistic Satanic groups out there, so you may be wondering why I didn't just join one of those. Unfortunately, theistic groups can be dangerous, particularly for women, with some linked to neo-Nazism. I also think many theistic Satanic groups suffer with the same confusion I myself had, in which they are not as certain about things as they pretend to be. Why if you truly believe in hell would you want to go there?

Now having been a Satanist and an agnostic one may seem an odd stance, but I think it had the virtue of being an honest one. There are many people from all religions who could say that there are gaps and wrinkles in their faith but who don't dare to confront them. Instead of acknowledging their misgivings they come across as totally ardent, hiding their doubts behind a facade of piety. I understand this because in the past I was similar, wanting to believe the Christian doctrine while feeling an attraction to the other side, and as a result I must have appeared fervent and devout.

Call me a cynic, but I suspect that the popularity of organised religion is due to this kind of internal conflict. It works like this: someone high up in whatever religion you choose to picture says that they experienced a miracle, or that their spell worked. Other people within the group hear this news and start to feel inadequate. Why has this not happened to them? So to soothe this pain, the people who feel inadequate start to attribute minor successes in their lives to miracles or magic. They then share their stories widely, which in turn makes others in the group feel they are also missing out.

The cycle continues, and you end up with a church full of blessings rather than a church full of people who acknowledge that things haven't worked out the way they'd been led to believe.

That's why I maintain that it is precisely the existence of hidden doubt which leads people to a more fervent state of belief, with their unacknowledged misgivings making them wish harder for religious teachings to be true. I think of this as the religious feedback loop.

I was caught in the religious feedback loop myself, but with a twist. I was unwavering on the outside, but on the inside I was never able to self-deceive. If something happened that seemed magical I'd always examine it closely, asking myself if there was a rational explanation. All the while I projected the image of certainty, appearing to others as they expected me to be. Yet I'd often wonder to myself if I'd got it all wrong, perhaps if I was more powerful or had the right spell books, could I achieve the results that other people claim to have achieved? There was always the notion in the back of my mind of what if there were people doing what I wished I could do. This is the nature of the religious feedback loop.

The reason I had such a strong desire for the Christian mythos to be true, especially with respect to hell, may be because I'm a masochist. Maybe masochist is not the correct term, because although I enjoy masochistic fantasies, I do not desire pain. But in my head, where I am in control, psychological torture—like the pain inflicted by my many bullies—can become fantasy material. The same can be said of physical pain; in my mind I can enjoy it. This however does not mean I enjoyed the experience of being bullied. I abhorred what people did to me in reality, and do not think that just because psychological torture can become fantasy material, this makes such bullying behaviour right. The same can be said of rape. Even if the victim has previously had fantasies about rape, it doesn't make it right to go out and rape that person. There is a big gulf between a fantasy where you are in control and a reality where you are not.

I have often reflected that my masochistic tendencies are the likely result of all the bullying I have suffered. In the face of intolerable pain, my mind has turned my suffering into a fetish to protect me from the hurt, anguish and damage inflicted by my bullies.

In the mortal world physical pain and psychological anguish come with material consequences. There are scars that don't heal, and mortality to worry about. This for me is where medieval depictions of hell come into play. I enjoy the idea of hell existing, because in those realms physical and psychological pain must have no lasting consequences, otherwise the punishment inflicted there could not be eternal.

The world of hell represents my freedom. While I fantasise about pain, I have never felt free to indulge my fetish in real life, for fear of mortal consequences.

Admittedly my vision of hell has changed a lot since being ill with schizophrenia. I expect if there is indeed a hell, then going there would be more like having never-ending schizophrenia than the tortures depicted in medieval imagery. If you have ever suffered with this illness, you will understand very well what kind of torment it is. Another reason I wanted Christian-style demons to exist is because I love the stories surrounding them. The stories connected to religious thought are my favourite thing about theology. Conversely, these stories are the part I believe in the least, as I see them as human interpretations of the metaphysical and natural world.

I love the idea of there being entities that manipulate the world of mankind, but of course I don't know for certain if these entities exist, or if they are so closely concerned with the affairs of humankind. My desire to believe in a Christian cosmos while also having had respect for an atheistic take on Satanism has caused me a lot of internal struggle. How could it not?

During my stay at university I never let people get too close to me, which was a useful part of my subterfuge, as it meant people wouldn't get close enough to ask me about my beliefs. I wasn't as sure of what I believed back then, and I knew if people asked me, my fear of telling outright lies would cause me to tell the truth. This would damage my carefully constructed fantasy world, and stop me giving people what they expected. A lot of my modus operandi was about being taken seriously, so admitting that I wasn't totally sure about anything would, I thought, cause people to laugh at me. I was never evil, or at least I didn't see myself that way. I was essentially harmless, an insect wearing warning colours to pretend it is dangerous.

Another facet of the image I projected, was the fear of disappointing people, I didn't want people to be disappointed if I told the truth about Satanism. I realise now that the type of people who would be disappointed by the truth about Satanism (myself included), are simply fetishising it, and they don't want their fantasy vision deconstructed. I didn't want to disappoint myself, so I lived through the eyes of others who knew nothing of the truth.

Many of you at Storthes Hall Student Village, where I lived, will have seen my window lit by a red light, with the infamous words HELL HERE stuck to the glass. My first-year flat was three storeys up, so I felt free to do this, knowing people wouldn't be able to see in as they would have if I had been on the ground floor. I displayed the sign because I saw my room as an extension of my personality, and I wanted you to feel my presence. Being omnipresent was a route to power.

The words HELL HERE represented many things to me. They revealed my name and communicated my desire to be discovered: Hell Here, Helen Here, this is my room, seek me out if you dare. The words also spoke of the depression I was feeling at the time.

Despite my desire to be mysterious, I could also feel lonely, and wanted people to know where I could be located.

My differences made connecting with others hard. The words on the window also served to make it apparent that my red light, which I always kept on during the night, was not an indicator that I was selling myself.

The idea behind these words came from one of the old Batman films, the one with Cat Woman. In the film, Cat Woman has a neon sign reading Hello There, and in the course of the narrative she smashes the sign, leaving it reading Hell Here. This scene entered my mind when I was wondering what words to put on my window.

The only curveball I threw into what was otherwise a very clichéd image was that I often listened to classical music instead of the heavy metal often associated with Satanism. I have loved classical music since I was young, having adored Disney's Fantasia, and I made sure you all were aware that this was the music I preferred, purely because I wanted you to know I wasn't just a complete Satanic cliché.

Thus you'd hear me playing loudly from my open window the music of Vangelis, Verdi's requiem, Mozart's requiem, Beethoven's piano sonatas, Philip Glass, Jeff Wayne's War of the Worlds, Jerry Goldsmith, various Gregorian chants and Vivaldi's four seasons. I did sometimes listen to Marilyn Manson, Cradle of Filth and Insane Clown Posse, but most often I preferred classical music.

I'd usually play music till three in the morning, because in my muddled mind three AM was a respectful time to turn it off to allow people to sleep. Partly this choice of timing was due to me thinking students would be partying till three AM and that it wouldn't affect anybody.

The fact that I was getting ill played a huge part in my

behaviour, and some of you might remember my blank passionless stare, which I found out later was a product of my illness. When people would throw insults, or shout at me, I'd fix them with this stare rather than shouting back, because to me shouting was not a classy way to behave. I am also not good at coming up with witty comebacks when confronted by hostility, so staring seemed the best way to deal with this, showing you I was confident enough to look you in the eyes.

Another thing about me that people must have found strange was that I appeared not to sleep. Not being able to sleep is a symptom of paranoid schizophrenia, so my constant walking round Storthes Hall in the dead of night was due to the fact I was trying to tire myself out in the hope of getting some quality sleep. I thought that if I wore my body out, my brain might fall asleep. This, unfortunately, never worked.

As a child I always had trouble sleeping, whether because of fear of the dark, constant nightmares, or the sleep paralysis I often suffered, but I'd always managed to get some sort of sleep. It was around the age of fifteen that I noticed my sleep getting worse. I would lie down in bed and suddenly I'd feel too excited to sleep, buzzy almost. I always describe the sensation to people as the way a child feels on the night before Christmas, that adrenaline rush and excitement, except I had no reason to feel excited. I'd also suffer with racing thoughts, a symptom of schizophrenia that causes the thoughts to tumble over one another quickly and with no clear path. The feeling is almost as if your mind is flickering, and you can't stay on topic. The best image I can conjure up is that of a flickering film reel inside your head. This symptom also prevents the sufferer from sleeping. My inability to sleep was the reason for my night-time meanderings.

Despite keeping people away from me, the illness made me very conflicted and contrary. I'd alternate between wanting to be alone and wanting company. I sometimes wanted to be seen as more normal instead of mysterious, and felt simultaneously powerful yet weak. Wanting not to be alone caused me to sit in the on-site TV lounge, or under a tree, making myself readily available to the curious. I did make a few friends this way in my first year, but for various reasons these friendships did not last.

Being ill and not knowing I was ill probably caused me to think I was a bigger sensation than I actually was. I was still hearing voices, and thought people were constantly discussing me. This is the sad thing about all the types of schizophrenia: the sufferer does not know they are ill, and does not seek help. Help often comes only when other people realise something is amiss.

On the bus rides to and from university I'd always sit on the luggage rack, mainly as a way of avoiding people, to prevent any of you sitting next to me. Peoples' fears of me may have prevented this anyway, but this never occurred to me. I'd often stare around the bus thinking people were whispering about me.

There was a time, during my first year, when I thought I heard the people who lived on the same floor as me talking about me outside my door. They were discussing how much they hated me, saying that I was like something from The Exorcist. Normally this wouldn't have bothered me, but on this occasion I felt very upset, and I rang my mum, crying, telling her people didn't like me. Looking back, I know now that the voices I heard could have been just that: voices.

I suspected the people who shared the floor with me in my first year thought I was on drugs. One night I told a girl from the room next to mine of a hallucination I'd had. I'd drifted off to sleep and abruptly woken up, and there on my ceiling was a large splatter of blood. I panicked while I looked and repeated over and over "It's not real". I was so shaken up that I immediately left my room and told someone about it. It was only afterwards that I realised I told my next-door neighbour about the incident without any context, and later was worried that she might have thought I'd had a drug-induced hallucination.

Schizophrenia is often thought of as an illness induced by drugs, but it is only in some cases that this is true. Often people with schizophrenia who also take drugs are doing so as a form of self-medication, using the drugs to try and reduce their distressing symptoms. I was never the type to want to take drugs, fearing the idea of being out of control of my own body.

On one occasion in mid-2006 I walked up to a girl who I thought was talking about me, and said to her in a spiteful tone "Stop talking about me!" She looked hurt and said she hadn't been. At the time it never occurred to me that she was walking quietly by herself when I 'heard' her. There were a few incidences of a similar type, but for most part I dodged the bullet of showing myself up in public. However, in 2006, in my second year at university, people would have seen me practising gymnastics and taekwondo outside my flat. I was in a very bad place then.

All in all, though, my first year at uni went okay. I was quite happy and full of myself, going through times of sadness but also enjoying times of fun. It was in my second year when the psychosis phase of schizophrenia really took hold.

Letter to the Voices: Part Two
Storthes Hall
May/June 2006

The Rumour

I woke up and heard a rumour spreading in the night,
something they said about me.
I was ecstatic with delight.

Not the sort of reaction a rumour should warrant,
I thought it would enhance my reputation.
Turns out it wouldn't.

This was in the beginning before things turned sour.
A schizophrenic delusion,
would sap me of my power.

I'd hear it rolling round the grounds of where I lived.
Thrilled people took me seriously,
that I could be Scary Mary.

Your fear was my delight.

You were very cruel to me during my stay at university, though it didn't start off as if you were being mean. I actually liked it when you insinuated I'd had sex with Satan. Of course, I didn't behave as a normal person might when confronted with this idea. I became excited, instead of (as an ordinary person might be) mortified. I thought such a rumour would enhance my scary, gothic reputation around Storthes Hall.

Throughout my illness you had a penchant for rumour making, and I didn't always like what you were saying.

I think of the time you uttered the statement "Oh my God, she's having sex with Satan!" as the beginning of the psychosis phase of the schizophrenia, as if you had been absent beforehand. Of course, you hadn't seemed as real back then, not as pervasive, but you had been there, whispering in my mind.

The first time I heard this rumour was one night when I had woken up from a brief interlude of sleep. When I first heard these words I became excited that 'real' people might think I copulated with demons, and you enabled these thoughts by pretending to be students who'd been scared when they had seen this happening. In my head I wondered how you could have possibly seen such a thing, because I knew it hadn't happened. But I took your mistake as being caused by the glow of my red light and shadows cast by moonlight filtering through my open curtains.

The rumour, as I thought it, wasn't real. It was all your illusion, and my broken mind believed it, fell for it. Such a rumour never circulated, and there were no students saying this about me. They were probably all in bed asleep, but to me you were actual people. The delusional state made me think you were real, possibly bored, students who had decided to spy on me that night through my window from a flat not quite opposite to my room. I thought that these students had been seeing shadows and making visual mistakes.

My deluded mind made it impossible for me to realise that I wouldn't have been able to hear people from the offending block, even if someone had shouted in that flat. And besides, you were all talking in whispers. I heard your voices, male and female, discussing the rumour amongst yourselves, debating "Could it possibly have happened?" When I heard such doubts cast upon the validity of the rumour, I became distressed and upset, and decided I should do something to sway things in my favour. I liked tasting your fear and became excited when I heard the horror and awe in your voices at the possibility of the rumour being true.

I'm ashamed of what I decided to do next, but of course it must be explained, or else what comes after makes little sense. In the days that followed I tried to exacerbate the rumour. I didn't do this by going around spreading the story myself, which to me felt too blatant to work, but by playing noise music in my flat, making it seem as if weird, otherworldly portals were being opened in my room. Or at least that is how I perceived it. This was probably nothing real people would have noticed, but the music seemed to convince you, my torturers, and the rumour in the form I wanted it appeared to spread.

Did people seem more afraid of me as I swanned around Storthes Hall? To me it seemed that way. Though I could still hear some of your voices casting doubts, and this irked me, most of you appeared to believe in the rumour, a belief which I equated to believing in me. In the summer I'd lie on the grass in the sun and listen to you discussing the topic, feeling excited about what I perceived as people's fears of me.

Yet, as I learned to my cost, my games would come at a price which was too high. Unaware I'd already lost my mind, I was about to lose my happiness, my dignity and my will. Was this all part of your plan?

O Sweet malice
flood down upon everyone
who is not me
For I am god

A Letter to Lucifer
Doncaster
2002-2023

Hell

You know those medieval pictures? The ones with all the fires.
They're sending all the traitors there, especially all the liars.

In masochistic revelry, I used to love that imagery.
They all seemed so dark to me, (so serious a fantasy).

Until I realised there's a greater Hell inside of me.
A darkness within, as you will later see.

For me (now) Hell would be.
Trapped in my room at university.

Hearing forever more, that tirade of voices.
Taking away my options and leaving me with no choices.

Trapped in my mind forever more.
With delusions inside, and voices outside my door.

The red light bearing down like a flame.
The constant anguish, and all that fame.

The owls and the crows.
The howls and the throes.
The hallucinating dread.
The wishing I were dead.
Breaking down and crying.
Apologising to the voices.
For all my lying.

Like demons in my head.
A possession that I bred.

My former view of Hell has changed
now my visions completely rearranged.

Hell (now), would be a darker place for me.
Than any infantile imagery.

And though those pictures are still quite fun.
A different vision madness has spun.

It seems almost irrelevant to write to you now, but there are still things that need to be said.

I've moved on so much that my original book is out of date, I was reluctant to do a rewrite, but I have changed. It's almost as if the last vestiges of my illness have been shed. I never intended to change, and never thought I would. I suffered from the end of history delusion, believing I would never change and that I'd remain static.

I was never certain that you existed, the only version of you that was really real to me was the vision of you that I created.

Back when I was fifteen I drew your picture. I drew you how I imagined you might look. The pencil drawing was not the perfect image, because I got the angle of your hand wrong when I did the foreshortening of your arm reaching towards the audience. The audience was usually me, because I often used to sit before your picture and voice my thoughts to the drawing of you, like a verbal diary of what was going on in my life, and what I thought and interpreted from such events. When I was alone, I preferred talking aloud to keeping a diary, because I did not want people intruding on my thoughts, especially with having two sisters around.

The image I drew of you was gaunt and pale skinned, with

long, straight, white, hair and clawed hands, feathered wings, horns and a deliberately false smile. You always wore white robes. The iris of your undamaged eye was white. Originally you were meant to have two working eyes, but I made a mistake, and the smudge of the eraser left one eye blind. I quite liked the effect, so I kept it that way. In this picture you look like a more masculine and fair-haired version of me. In this drawing I think I was expressing love for myself as much as the love I had for you.

I believe the drawing I made of you was an exploration of my own sexuality, based on the visuals I liked. I even gave you a dark personality, informed by what I have read of devils, and by what my fantasies found enticing.

It is hard for me to write these words, because when it comes to talking about my sexuality to anybody but myself—and of course, in the past, your picture—I am very shy about it. There is almost a Victorian prudishness in me when it comes to talking about sex. This is probably because some of my sexuality seems deviant when compared to the mainstream. I guess now it is no secret that my sexual preference is for demons, at least in fantasy. My physically unexplored masochism is what makes devils alluring to me, I suppose.

Another aspect of my demon fetish is the fear of my own sexuality. The domineering vision I created for you was a good way to project my own sexual desires onto someone else. In my head you were the one in control, so I could project my proclivities onto you, this was a good way to avoid ownership of them, instead of it being me that enjoyed the torture, it was you, it was almost as if I created you to compartmentalise my sexuality, so that I could not confront myself with it.

The reason I feel the need to do this is unclear, what I am aware of is this, for a very long time I was afraid of sex, despite the fact I have never been abused in that way.

I desperately tried to separate myself from my own sexuality, and tried hard to avoid being seen as sexual to others. The thought of being in a situation where sex might really happen, frightened me, I however didn't mind people fetishising me because of my religion, because they weren't really judging me on any of my human attributes, but rather their own fantasy vision of what I might be like.

The way I used my fantasy world and vision of you was almost like a self aware split personality, but instead of you being a separate personality that I became, I consciously used you as a way of reflecting on things that I didn't dare confront myself.

Intellectually I know there is nothing unnatural about sex, but it's as if this knowledge doesn't translate into my emotions, so I still feel a deep shame and guilt over my human nature. It's as if I feel it shouldn't be talked about, I never wanted people to perceive me as human because that would mean I have all the weaknesses of the human condition.

I spent a lot of time and energy eradicating my humanness, making sure to appear ethereal, Satanic, unearthly and inhuman.

I did a lot of micro-managing of my image so that I could control people's perceptions of me.

The need for control in my life is what made the biblical version of you appealing. I wanted to be seen as evil or as a devil because I saw the imagery of you as having unquestioned power and control, you being the most magically powerful in your realm. My desire to be seen as evil was basically me trying to expand my fantasy world into the real world. My masochistic desires are, I suspect, also related to control. Throughout my life I've spent so much time trying to subtly control the world and peoples' views of me that I have a need to unwind in fantasy, where I imagine relinquishing control or having no control in the first place.

I also think that who we are in our fantasies is often the opposite to who we are in reality. A child will fantasise about being a superhero because they are looking for strength, control, and a bravery they feel they lack. In my fantasies I used to fantasise about causing revolutionary trouble in hell, which inevitably got me punished by demons. In these fantasies I was always resisting, and I was not afraid to speak up.

My reality looked very different. There, I tended to stick to rules, tended to shy away from argument, and behaved in a diplomatic manner. I was often quiet about my opinions, afraid of causing turmoil—even at times when I felt I really should say something—and I hardly ever voiced my opinion on the internet.

As I have become better at speaking up and expressing my own opinions the need for these fantasies has waned, as I become more able to control my own life the need for you slowly dissipates.

After I was ill, when I was recovering I tried not to fantasise at all because I was too embarrassed and knew my fantastical inner-world had led me astray and caused me to do incredibly stupid things. Even just fantasising in a more general way was something I couldn't bring myself to do. I can now enter my inner world again but it has changed a lot.

Another important motivation for my interest in demons, I believe, is the strength of my death drive, or Thanatos. The death drive is, in Freudian psychological theory, our desire to destroy ourselves, to find the shortest possible route to the primeval condition of death. It is in constant opposition to Eros, the life drive. The death drive is expressed through acts of violence directed at others or ourselves, including self-destructive behaviours. Eros, on the other hand, manifests as the desire to procreate, to protect one another, to stay alive and continue the species. I believe strongly in the Eros vs. Thanatos theory of the human psyche because I feel these forces so acutely in myself.

I have a strong life drive. In my physical body I tend to avoid psychological and physical harm. However, I am also aware of a strong opposing pull of Thanatos which seems to centre upon my soul and which is played out in my fantasy life. My self-destructive side doesn't seek to destroy me in a physical way, but rather seeks to exist in the fantasy of constant suffering. Suffering gives me clarity and something to resist, to fight against, without the fight having to be physical. This is why visions of medieval hell seem alluring to me. Of course, I appreciate happiness and contentment as well, but suffering is what gives me a sense of purpose. Though I will point out suffering is only alluring in hindsight, because when a person is actually suffering it is really quite awful.

However suffering makes things happen and motivates change, for if a person is unhappy the are likely to seek to change it, which is why when conditions get worse for the majority of people there is likely to be a revolution.

It will come as no surprise to you that I often wonder about the nature of pain. The existence of pain is a mystery which causes me to favour agnosticism over atheism. Pain is, as we all know, a great teacher. It stops us from sticking our hands in the fire and damaging our bodies. Pain instils fear, and the association between pain and fear is what stops antelopes mingling with lions and becoming food. Pain drives us to continue our species, for if we fear pain we fear death, and we seek to escape it. But that raises the question of why we have a drive to survive. Who is out there rooting for us?

When I was becoming ill, I was very excited about you and about Satanism. I used to think upon the subject every day and ponder different ideas about religion. If I thought hard about you I used to feel as though I had an invisible thread connecting me to you. I could literally feel it coming from my heart and disappearing off into the ether. I think this feeling could have been related to getting ill, and perhaps I was thinking along the lines of the invisible thread that is said to tether the soul to the body in out-of-body experiences. Or perhaps there was something true in my experience. I guess while I'm alive I can never know.

I brought the picture of you to university and put it on my wall. I had to be more careful about talking to you at university than I had at home because I didn't want people to hear me, especially since I was talking about my personal thoughts. When I talked to your picture I'd almost see you reacting to what I was saying. I'd think about whether you were amused, or if you looked angry. Although it sounds strange to say it, I saw you as a companion. Anton LaVey mentions artificial companions in one of his writings, and this idea resonated with me when I read it because I had felt such connections for myself, even before my relationship with your picture.

Growing up I had a few artificial companions that I'd relate to. I had a poster of Team Rocket as a child—I liked the antagonists from Pokémon and used to talk to them—and I went through a phase where Snape from Harry Potter was someone I spoke to regularly. At one point I even had conversations with a picture of a character in a computer game manual. In my mind, as with your picture, I'd always see them reacting to what I was saying. These characters were all ones that I respected, whether this was due to traits they had that I deemed cool, or because they were interesting.

I never had posters of celebrities or other people I wouldn't want to look at me, because I have this strange feeling that pictures staring into our world can see me. I guess the closest thing to this feeling is the sense of a painting's eyes following the viewer round a room, though of course my mind took this illusion and ran with it. I suspect I have the tendency to relate to pictures so intensely because I did not have many friends growing up, so I developed the ability to find my friends elsewhere.

I feel bad that I fell out with your picture after I was ill. This happened because later in my illness, while I was apologising to you for all I believed I'd done, I saw your likeness pulling faces at me. This experience motivated me to put away the picture for quite some time. It was only years later that I got the drawing out again. I used to talk to your picture a lot, I understand that other people might view my behaviour as very odd, but I saw it as a form of introspection. Talking to you helped me get my own thoughts in order. I still talk out loud but I talk to myself, there is no reason I couldn't talk to you except that it makes me feel Satanic, and I've moved on from that now.

One of the reasons I opt to paint pictures instead of writing things down is because words are dangerous. Once they are written down they are there for all to see, even if you later change your opinions. A painting is less explicit. It can be interpreted in myriad ways and doesn't explicitly tell people what you think. Writing this story is a frightening act for me. It exposes so many things about my deepest self, even though I've chosen to unearth them. Words are very dangerous.

A Letter to Amy
Doncaster
1992-Present

Our Animal Games

I have no idea how we met, why we met. Yet here we are, painted in stars, baring our scars.
Where are those days when we were young, fun and more or less carefree? I don't see how time could have moved on so quickly.

Thirty years on, that time has gone, far distant from our animal games.

I may have this entirely wrong, but I felt that when I was getting ill we drifted apart a little. You are my oldest and best friend. I've known you since I was four or five, and time erodes the exact memory of our meeting.

We always played together, mostly pretending to be anthropomorphic animals. Sometimes we were mixtures of different animals with superpowers, depending on what the game called for. The only boundaries we had were the limits of our imaginations.

I recollect how we used to explore abandoned houses, making up ghost stories to go with these buildings. I'd most often wait outside while you and the others went in. I wasn't afraid of the stories we told, but of something much more earthbound; I was frightened the police would catch us and tell us off. I knew that were weren't supposed to be exploring the houses and was more finickity about this than you.

One of our stories surrounding an abandoned house was the

story of the ghost cat. It was a story about how a millionaire owned all the houses on a particular street, and how he went crazy and strangled a cat in the bathtub. We were young, of course, and didn't realise that a millionaire probably wouldn't live in a humble terraced house in Doncaster.

And do you remember the time we got caught hiding in the evergreen trees at the back of an old man's garden? We'd meant no harm, but were always sneaking in there to play, because the dense trees suited our animal games. Then one day the old man caught us, and we screamed. Getting into the old man's garden was something we made into an adventure, using walkie talkies and telling each other if the coast was clear.

I still cherish the memory of Greendale Animal Village, our epic saga of a game. Each break time at school, we'd run outside and do the theme song, complete with theme dance, then continue with our narrative, moving the story on from the last time. My character in that game was a cat. I'd often play as the main character, preferring to keep the same pretend creature, whereas you'd change things up and play every character around me. Perhaps it was the thespian in you that made you try out different roles. By contrast I was always a very static person, usually being happy with what I'd decided, and not feeling the need for change.

Primary school was a mixed bag for both of us. We both suffered the cruel taunts of our peers, purely for the crime of being different. They would often call us lesbians, and in typical childlike fashion we didn't think to realise there would have been nothing wrong with it if we had been. Being bullied affected me tremendously, and it is only in hindsight that I realised the impact it had. Inwardly I was very confident, so it was never the content of what the bullies said that hurt me, I never believed I was stupid or ugly or awful in any way. I just didn't believe them when they said these things. However, what did hurt was the injustice. Specifically, the fact that I knew I didn't deserve the bullying I received.

The way in which this bullying has impacted me is that even today I have a mistrust of people. I don't like loud, aggressive voices or tones, or aggressive words. My heart races when I pass gangs of teenagers, especially if they dress like my school bullies, or if they are being very noisy. My tendency is to look for danger everywhere. Being invited to new places with new people did frighten me, though I am getting over this now. I also get nervous about committing to anything, for fear of authority, and my nervousness increases when dealing with officialdom. I know the bullying has affected you as well, and I also know that you didn't have the same reassuring inner voice as me, telling you that you weren't a bad person.

In primary school I often got the impression that you were jealous of me, which was the source of some of our childish arguments. You'd try to do things to make me jealous of you. I remember that you would often copy my drawings, to my annoyance. I wanted my drawings to be unique, and you'd try do better than me. I realise now that the lack of self-esteem you felt was probably what motivated you.

I rarely got jealous on these occasions. I rarely feel jealous these days, in fact. I have experienced the emotion before, while I was young, like a twisting feeling in my chest. But perhaps due to the illness, or maybe the medication, a lot of my emotions have disappeared or don't affect me as much. These days I feel as though I'm processing emotions in my head rather than my heart. It's not so much that I never get jealous, embarrassed or angry, it's more that I know what I'm experiencing, but I don't feel the emotion connected to it. It was only during the psychosis stage of schizophrenia that my emotions became overly intense. This deficit doesn't affect all my emotions: I still feel excitement, sadness, fear and love. But I sometimes wonder if the overly intense emotions I felt while ill with schizophrenia burned out my circuits.

One of the reasons I feel we stuck together as friends is because we were so different. I'm a great believer that opposites attract. You were always more emotional than me, and I was often more stoic. I liked you because you were able to break the rules, and you were more overtly confident on the outside than me. I got the feeling you admired me for my imagination and inner confidence. In turn I admired you for always being able to say how you felt about things, whereas I always stuck to a diplomatic approach, even if I was being insulted.

My favourite primary school teacher, and I think yours too, was Mr Sheckle. It was in his classes that I was most productive, and those were the times when I feel I had the most light in me. Mr Sheckle always encouraged and nurtured my talents, and I'd often spend my breaktime indoors in the classroom, writing poems and illustrating them. Even if they weren't particularly good poems, I felt that my artistic creativity and enthusiasm for learning were much appreciated by this teacher.

It was around this age that I started becoming interested in psychology. My interest began when I started to speculate about the feelings of students who were raising their hands to answer questions in class. I was pondering, at this time, about how the students would react emotionally in different scenarios. It was this early interest in psychology that led me to the deep understanding I now have of myself, because anything I felt I would probe, with no denial of having felt it. If I felt angry or sad, I would ask myself why, and explore what was wrong. This ability came with one disadvantage or advantage, depending on your point of view: I became unable to deceive myself.

Nothing that crosses my mind is hidden from me. I feel as if things bypass my subconscious and I have immediate access to them, which makes me acutely aware of any failings on my part. The advantage is that I can immediately have access to my feelings and reason them out, rather than letting my heart and emotions take charge. This makes me slower to react emotionally to things. I feel this ability comes from my practice of talking to myself and previously to my various artificial companions, because speaking out loud meant I could get my thoughts in order and find patterns and nuances to my thinking and behaviour.

I would recommend this kind of self-reflection to anyone, because reacting less instinctively to scenarios helps deal with them in a sensible manner. I may sometimes feel hurt by people's words, but not letting my emotions take over means I won't reflexively hurt the person back. Instead, I can see possible reasons why they might think or say such things, and appreciate when these are not related to me.

As we got older and into secondary school it was deemed inappropriate to play our games, especially to run on all fours like an animal, so I stopped doing this. I remember how we used to come up with plans to get back at our bullies, plans we knew could never work, and schemes we wouldn't dare to try. But it was fun to pretend we would do these things. Once we made a ball out of the wax encasing Babybel cheese and filled it with all sorts of things. We had planned to pretend it was chewing gum and give it to our worst bully at the time in the hope of making her ill. Of course, we didn't go through with our plan.

As we entered our teenage years, I started to express an interest in witchcraft, which made you nervous. You'd tell me that it was a bad idea and share horror stories with me from Shout magazine about kids who'd meddled in witchcraft and had bad stuff happen to them. And indeed I suppose you could say, after looking at what happened to me, that bad stuff did happen.

You were one of the few people I trusted enough, later on, to share the secret that I was into Satanism, even though you were alarmed by my new-found interest. Your alarm barely registered, because by then I was so strongly compelled by the idea of Satan that no-one's disapproval could have stopped me anyway. Whether this was due to the illness taking hold I don't know, but the emotions I was feeling about Satan were so strong and irresistible that it would only take me seeing a word related to him on a page of a book to cause a spike in adrenaline and a strange buzz.

I understand now how worrying my behaviour must have been. At the time I had no outlet for my desires, and all I could do to express them was act in a dark and brooding manner. It was only when I found the literature of LaVey that my Satanic inclinations found a real direction. You wouldn't have known this though, because I didn't let people know the truth about myself or the LaVeyan variant of this religion. Instead I made it appear as though I was evil, but in secret much of what LaVey said made sense to me. In my experiments with finding evil, I didn't think about the impact I was having on those around me, and I never revealed my hand, not even to you. I feel nowadays that this was the wrong thing to do. You are my best friend after all, and I knew that you wouldn't have laughed at me. But I was so terrified that people wouldn't take me seriously as a Satanist if I told the truth. So I only told myself the truth.

Throughout all my dark experimentation we remained friends. We never really discussed the Satanism, and you were always there supporting me through the torment of being bullied. In my later school career, most people knew that I was a Satanist, in part because I wanted them to know. I hadn't directly told anyone, but when I was asked by a student in form room, before lessons, whether the rumours were true, I gave a very unconvincing "No." This was part of my plan. I reasoned that if people came to know about my Satanism through the grapevine, I would be blameless, not having told them directly.

Later in my time at school, just before we broke up for the summer holidays, I did directly come out and tell a boy in our year that the rumours about my religion were true. He looked shocked when I told him, and I saw my confession as going out with a bang. This was the year before we started sixth form.

As I moved into the sixth form I became very self-obsessed and arrogant, largely due to my steadily worsening mental health. It was around this time that you drew back a little. But then who could blame you? Even if you weren't as close to me then, you were resolutely there for me after my illness was diagnosed.

It was my behaviour, I think, that put you off. We were still friends, but I had the sense that you were worried about me, and perhaps a little scared too. My behaviour was quite erratic and exuberant, and I used to behave oddly, doing things that seemed random and strange but that made sense to me. I'd sit or lie on the backs of the sofas, chase people around threatening to curse them, and once got extremely angry and threatened to kill someone when I realised he'd stolen from me.

We had a gang of friends in the common room, who sat in what we termed 'the nerdy corner'. There was Andy, Myers, Carla, Alan, Abbey, Steph, Nicola, Ryan, John and Emma, amongst others. Yet despite having all these friends, I felt largely alone. I believed that you, Ryan Emma, John, and Andy where the only ones that really wanted me around. I felt as if the whole gang really liked you, but that I was on the fringes of the group. This feeling could have been teenage angst, or perhaps the feelings of isolation brought about by my differences to others.

To be fair, I spent half of my time play-acting to people in the common room, trying to frighten and intrigue in equal measure. I often felt that I was only really a member of the group because I was your friend, and I often wondered if you felt closer to Carla than me at this point. None of this was your fault. I was too far into my own little world, building up an elaborate fantasy realm that I imposed upon others. I spent far too much time scaring the other students and creating an image of evil than I spent cultivating my own friendships. You were also probably dealing with your own issues at the time, which I would not have been aware of.

I used to get invited to parties held by our friendship group, but convinced myself that they only invited me to make up numbers, or because I was your friend, so I wouldn't get offended at not having an invite, much like the fairy from Sleeping Beauty. Nowadays I get on well with a lot of this group and have gotten closer to some people that I used to not know as much about. The group has morphed and changed over the years as well, gaining new members and losing others.

I was completely unaware that I was going insane around this time. The only reason I know I am ill now is because of the medication I take. The medicine quiets the voices in my head and takes away the delusions I had. Though I had some voices at school which I thought were people discussing me, I didn't yet have any delusions, or at least none that stuck. I knew what I was doing, and at this point I wasn't motivated by delusion, but was motivated by the intense excitement I got from scaring people, and from the buzz my religion gave me.

As you know, at school I had no sexual relationships, or even romantic ones. This was largely because I saw myself as asexual, and the idea of having sex scared me. I think I feared the pain the first time might bring. I was not ready, and the illness made me feel disinterested in people. I think my repressed sexuality was sublimated into religious ardour. What I wasn't doing sexually, I put into my fervency and my apparently solid conviction in myself.

I think part of my image was about communicating the idea that I was a non-sexual being. I dressed in an androgynous fashion, covering up all my femininity, and making myself appear as if I was of no gender. Recently I realised that my image was in part to escape the idea in other people's minds that I was a sexual being, as well as in my own mind. To admit to sexuality would make me like everyone else, and I had always felt a disconnect from humanity, as if I was not meant to be part of the human race. Although it sounds bleak, this was not a bad feeling. It made me happy.

Though I never actively fancied any of my peers, I did find I liked it when they appeared to fetishise me. I suspected that a few people fancied me because of my religious affiliation, and I would enjoy tormenting them specifically. One boy sat next to me while I was perched on the back of one of the common room sofas and tried to take a photo with me. I pushed him backwards off the sofa angrily saying, "I'm NOT a tourist attraction!" I worried after I'd done this that I'd face retribution from his friends for the action, but came to realise he had enjoyed the domineering way I treated him on that occasion.

While I was at university we fell out of touch, mostly due to me living in a dream world. I can't even remember if I ever called you for a conversation, except the conversation we had when I was very ill, and that was you calling me because my mum told you I was in distress. When you called me, I spilled out all my anger and anguish about how I was being bullied by the students at university. I was swearing and sounded upset, while you empathised with me and tried to calm me down. No-one back home knew I was ill at this point, because complaining I was being bullied was quite a normal thing for me. People were not near me at the time to see things going wrong, because my friends had gone to uni themselves or were back home in Doncaster. I'm sorry I did not nurture my friendships more back then.

The one phone call I can remember making was when I called you after I'd been medicated in April 2007. I called to tell you that I had not been bullied by the students at the university halls, but that I had been very ill with paranoid schizophrenia. My voice was quiet as I told you this, and emotionally I felt empty. You were massively upset for me and helped me through that difficult time. I needed a friend at that moment in my life, and you were there.

I hope you don't think less of me when you read this letter. It's been so hard to explain to anyone how I really viewed—and view—the world. It's taken me a long time just to come to terms with my belief system. While I was ill, I came across as so sure of myself, and created a persona of such conviction, that it feels hard to go back and say, "You know that person? She wasn't real. She was as unreal as the voices in my head".

A Letter to a Bloodletter
Storthes Hall
Oct 2005

Looking for Vampires

You were looking for me, and you found me.
You said you were looking for vampires,
having seen my gothic dress.
I didn't confess I was not that experienced,
and that I saw myself as a demon.

I was prideful and thought you could offer fame,
not the shame I feel when I think of our meeting.
The article in question, gave an impression
of me that was not quite real.

And anyway, I saw myself as a demon.

I feel I must put this event in a letter, because I have the sense that what happened is bound to come back and bite me.

There were many rumours about me while I lived at Storthes Hall, real rumours as well as those in my head. Why wouldn't there be? I came across as so different to everyone around me. I knew there was some real speculation, because the security staff, whom I often spoke to, would gleefully and spontaneously tell me what people had said about me.

The rumour about me drinking blood was one which was actually true. The rumour started after I told people in my flat that I'd tried someone's blood at a party in my pre-university years. My flatmates must have told people about my confession, which was how we ended up meeting. You knew of my existence before I knew of yours, and with my red light shining from my window you knew exactly where to find me.

So it was on a night in October that you knocked on my door with the express purpose of bloodletting and blood drinking. My paranoia about being pranked meant that I rarely answered the door to anyone without finding out who they were first. I asked who you were, from my position laid on my bed, and you gave me your name and told me what it was you wanted. My first instinct was to reply “No, come back another time. I'm tired!” and I sent you away without opening the door.

My blatant refusal came from my tiredness, as I'd barely slept for days, but mostly from my nervousness about the act of drinking blood, which overcame the need to indulge my fetish. I was inexperienced, and nervous at the thought of you taking my blood. I have never been the type to mutilate my own body, and I didn't know what you'd expect from me. You were clearly not someone who was playing a prank, so I knew sooner or later you'd turn up again.

The second time you turned up, I let you into my flat.

My curtains were open, and you turned the main light on when you entered. I have little recollection of what we talked about, except that you said you were depressed. We soon decided to get to the business for which you'd come. I picked up a blade I had in my room, that I'd acquired for cutting art paper. I passed it over to you and said harshly, “Be careful with me!”

You cut into my shoulder. It didn't hurt, but I felt faint at the thought of being damaged. After you had tasted my blood, it was my turn, the part I was more excited about. You made an incision, and I tasted your blood. I much preferred playing the predator.

After we had made this exchange, you then did something shocking, which I had not been expecting… you asked me to go out with you. I replied, "Sorry I don't go out with anyone." I was only interested in my own world, the world inside my head.

Picking up the blade again, obviously depressed at the rejection, you decided to draw more of your blood. But the blade was sharper than you realised, and you pressed it too hard into your skin. The flesh sprang apart down to the muscle.

"You didn't mean to do that." I said in a flat voice, totally inappropriate for the situation.

Though you were in pain, I continued to drink your blood, not thinking about the seriousness of the injury. I was probably just as shocked as you were.

You went into my bathroom to clean your wound. While you were in there, and while my hands were covered in your blood, two students came bursting in through the door, which I'd forgotten to lock after your arrival. I was usually meticulous about keeping my door locked, feeling that people's intrigue of me might make them want to get into my room. I was certainly proved right on this occasion. Perhaps the unusual fact of the main light being on had alerted people that something was going on in my room.

The two students saw me and exclaimed "Fucking hell." I advanced upon them hoping to scare them away, and then you came tearing out of the bathroom, with your wound wrapped in a bloodstained cloth. You shouted at the students, "Go away, she's not the devil." This, I thought, might have made them believe I was the devil.

I sent you away, hoping you could get help and I could get some sleep. You must have been in shock, because you mumbled something about sleeping it off. When you'd gone, I couldn't sleep anyway. The excitement of what had happened, coupled with the fact I knew you'd return made me restless.

When you came back I was unsurprised. The injury was bad, so we decided to get you to hospital. We went down to the security desk to ask them to call an ambulance, using the terrible excuse that you had been juggling knives and it had gone wrong. The security staff clearly didn't believe our story, but they called the ambulance anyway.

I didn't go with you, for which I now feel very cruel, because you had asked me to accompany you to the hospital. But by now I desperately wanted some sleep and didn't want to ruin my chances by spending hours in accident and emergency. Also, in the worsening mess of my mind, I didn't want you to think there was any chance of a relationship between us when I'd only wanted your blood.

As I was getting steadily more ill, my fantasies became more bloody and violent, and drinking blood featured in a lot of them. It was the dark nature of the act that appealed to me, and the sharing of someone's precious resource. The link to dark rituals and the violation of a taboo appealed to me sexually, giving me a predatory feeling at the idea of doing something others wouldn't do.

Being predatory appealed to me. All the things I wore were designed to make me appear less human, the claws, and horns, the wings, all designed to erase traces of anything that would make me appear mortal.

In the immediate aftermath of the bloodletting incident, because of the two students who ran into my room, I started to get the occasional feelings of paranoia, and the feeling of being watched. It was intermittent at this stage, but it would give me a creepy feeling whenever it happened. I started to become convinced that people would have good reason to want to watch my room. Yet despite this I never closed the curtains or changed my habits. I would devise plans of what I might do should someone enter my room again. One of these such plans was that I'd hide under my desk and shock the offending person by grabbing their leg.

Much later, well after this incident, a woman reporting for a magazine came up to me in the street. She'd seen my gothic dress, and said she'd been looking for vampires. I considered myself a demon but agreed to take part in an article on vampirism. She intended to pay me, which meant a lot on my student budget.

One thing interesting to note is that I've never actually been into vampires, despite my dress sense appearing that way, I was always into demons, vampires appearing too mortal. I never read any literature on them and despite desiring to drink blood, I was never all that interested in them.

I'm sure you'll understand that the existence of this magazine article is why I feel I need to write about our encounter. I regret taking part in the article because of its potential to affect my life and career, and your future.

I didn't mention your name in the article, but the interviewer did ask me if I'd ever drunk blood, and I'd told her about the incident. Much of the content in the article was changed, probably to simplify it for the flow of the narrative, so what I told the interviewer was very different from her final account. This disappointed me at the time, because I didn't want people thinking me a liar.

The interviewer must have found me strange, because I seemed to find the whole incident of blood drinking amusing. I know now that laughing out of turn and finding bizarre scenarios funny is yet another symptom of schizophrenia. At the time I kept reiterating that I was a demon, until the interviewer got frustrated and asked, "Are you happy to be called a vampire for the article?" I said I was, but my incoherent ramblings and odd behaviour must have worried and disconcerted her. I think she was glad to be shot of the interview afterwards.

I did the article because I was young, and I stupidly thought it might boost my art career. But the fact the article exists is my fault. I still feel responsible even though at the time I was deeply mentally ill. Sharing my story with a magazine was a bad move, and I'm terribly sorry if it has affected you in any way.

The existence of the article, should this book ever become well known, is why I felt the need to mention this part of my life. I'm taking ownership of it before anyone uses it against me.

It is important to note that I never engaged in blood drinking again after this incident. Once I'd tried it properly I decided the reality doesn't match the fantasy, as alluring something seems in fantasy sometimes it is best it stays in your imagination as the real life logistics are a lot more complicated.

A Letter to the Students on the Art Course
Huddersfield University
2005-2007

Fame

I'm going to be famous one day, I thought.
Buying into the dream we all had, when
we were but teenagers.

I felt it so keenly, I was so good,
there was no way I couldn't win,
knock knock let me in.

A door closes in my face.

I was a student of Fine Art. It's no surprise: my dress sense was in itself almost a work of art, and in a way my room in Storthes Hall became an art installation. One of my tutors said I was making myself into a one-dimensional character, something I was aware of and was perfectly happy about. Actually, the tutor in question was quite astute in terms of my image, though he seemed determined to change it without asking why I behaved as I did.

Like most people at the university, I don't think you knew what to make of me. Some of you did become friends, but my behaviour was disturbing to a lot of you.

I'd been an artist from a young age. As a child I taught myself to draw dragons and dinosaurs, and when I was older, I graduated to drawing demons and monsters. I once impressed my dad with a drawing of a thirty-headed dragon, each head unique. I liked designing imaginative ocean scenes because I was enchanted by fish, and at one point had a fascination with ocean sponges. I used to get cardboard boxes, tip them on their sides, and make dark jungle scenes within them, using glue and coloured paper. They'd have jagged grasses at the bottom, and vines hanging from the 'ceiling' of the box.

Once, in year four at school, I had the initiative to ask some builders who were replacing the mirrors in the girls' bathroom if I could have a piece of mirror to make a lake for a school project. Unfortunately, Mr Sheckle had to tell me the builders couldn't do this for health and safety reasons, so that project didn't quite come off.

I, as people can probably guess, was very imaginative. I was fifteen before I put my toys away, these were mostly dinosaurs and aliens from the Alien franchise. I used to spend hours in solitude making up games with my dinosaurs. The Jurassic Park Velociraptors were my favourite, and I often cast them as the baddies of the piece. I would use my red felt tip pens to make the characters look injured. I'd spend most of my time alone and had very little interest in the world around me. I knew almost nothing about what was going on politically and took more interest in the news if it was telling me about the next lunar eclipse.

My interest in my toys didn't fade as it does—I assume—for most children. One day when I was fifteen, I said to my mum "I feel weird about playing with toys," then put them away and never played with them again. I regret that I did this, because once you step outside of a childlike imagination it is hard to find a way back in. In my head I still made up games, mostly when I was awake at night unable to sleep. But I had put my toys away, thinking that I should grow up.

One of the more alarming things I did at university was creating fake wounds on my face. I feel this comes directly from making my toys look injured. As I became ill I steadily became fascinated with special effects, I enjoyed making my face paint look convincingly like blood and would make it look as though my eyes were bleeding. One of my more frightening effects was when I'd make it look as though the edge of my mouth was gashed open and held together with wire. No wonder I didn't make friends easily!

During university I had very specific views about what art was. My first criterion was that a work of art had to have meaning, some purpose to its creation. It had to be interesting, not a chocolate box picture of a cottage or something. And there had to be some effort involved. I always disliked art that was too simple, like a splat on a canvas selling for millions, or a banana taped to a wall.

Clever as the apparent ideas behind these types of art might be, I've often felt they're a con perpetrated by people who are already very wealthy and with the connections to get into a gallery, just to make themselves richer with minimal effort. If me in all my poorness were to suggest taping a banana to a wall of a gallery, they might think I was well… bananas.

These days, I'm less puritanical about my art tastes, though I still like to see some effort. I'm particularly inspired by outsider art, known in the art world as art brut. It is the kind of art which the creator never intended for a gallery wall, such as the art of the mentally ill, created while locked in an institution. This category includes art created by people fleeing war zones, folk art, and the art of children. I love this style because I feel the artists have so much more to say with their work, especially compared to the stale pieces that are often found in major galleries. Outsider art just feels more visceral and meaningful, perhaps because the intent was never for the art work to make money, so it's creators say exactly what they want to say, and don't stifle their vision to fit with what sells.

I do enjoy visiting big galleries, but I tend to find them very much of a muchness. There's a lot of sterile art in them that isn't allowed to say a lot and has no freedom of expression. This is because of the very narrow window of what is accepted into major galleries. There's a similar situation with music. There are lots of very visceral bands saying meaningful things, and who have very different sounds, but you won't find any of them in the hit parade. There is a certain sound that dominates the airwaves, and by definition it has a certain banality. There are particular narratives that prevail during different times, and if a person wants to part of the in-crowd, then they had better stick to the prevailing ideals of the time, lest they be thought of as not serious and a laughing stock. The primacy of certain ideological states is what causes works of mainstream art and music to appear very similar; if an artist is telling a story that is liked by the establishment, then they are more likely to be promoted to the top.

That is not to say I hate all artists that are exhibited in big galleries. I like Giger and Dalí, Frida Kahlo and Gordon Cheung, Andy Goldsworthy and Escher. I do like some of the old masters as well, particularly the apocalyptic biblical scenes they painted.

My behaviour in the art room at university was bizarre by any standards. I'd often make demonic screeching noises and would run round on all fours in crab fashion, with my stomach pointed towards the ceiling. I'd taught myself to move extremely fast this way. I could also run around fast on all fours like an animal, a relic from playing animal games as a child.

I'm sorry to say that a lot of you, my fellow students, merited my internal scorn. I felt that you didn't really know what you were doing with your art, whereas I had concrete ambitions and ideas, or at least thought I did. My projects were all about the realms of hell and religion. I produced paintings of dead worlds, with no weather patterns and dying foliage. Oil paints were my main medium, but I did use acrylics and pencils for some works. One work that I do remember creating was a piece titled "Don't Have Kittens". The drawing featured seven kittens on one side and the seven-headed beast of The Book of Revelation on the other side, with a prone figure at the front. Through this piece I was cynically wondering whether the author of Revelation was taking drugs at the time he wrote it.

A lot of my work centred on my nightmares, so Dalí's art was a major inspiration. As you will remember, I concentrated on dark themes, because happy memories didn't inspire me as much. I once read a quote that said, "Before you banish your inner demons, first make sure they are not the best part of you."

Later, in my second year with you, I started working on a project called Team Satan. I was getting quite ill and wasn't really sure why I was working on the project, though it allowed me to indulge my desire for props. For this project I made a creepy mummified doll, which I would carry around with me whilst wearing a black veil over my face. I made demon masks and a desiccated cat, and a creepy entity with no face, with spiders bursting from where its face should have been. The vague idea behind the project was that I wanted to put hell on earth, so was making these hellish props. But in my muddled state I couldn't articulate why I wanted to put hell on earth in the first place.

There was a comical aspect running through the project as well. The demon masks I made represented characters that were trying to sneak hell onto earth. There was a bit of a medical theme there too, based on the UK comedy series Green Wing, almost as if these props were being made in a medical lab in hell.

The idea I was trying to execute was a fantasy installation

with a conspiracy theme thrown in, in which demons were expanding hell onto Earth, sneaking items from their realm into ours. I also tried to make an accompanying book called the Rules of Engagement, which set out the rules which must be adhered to in the hidden war between heaven and hell. One of the rules was that angels and demons can only appear to people who won't be believed when they tell, like children or the insane, which looking back now was ironic. I had plenty of good ideas for sure, but I was very ill at this point so I couldn't quite put them into action.

The conspiracy element to the Team Satan project may have come from my teenage years. When I was thirteen, I was browsing the internet in class during some free time, and I stumbled across an article on black helicopters. These are, it was alleged, tiny helicopters which are grown in cows, and then burst out of their carcasses in a swarm. I don't know if my intense interest in the black helicopter conspiracy theory was because I was getting ill, or if it was because I was thirteen years old, new to the internet, and thought I'd stumbled upon some big secret. But I'd visit the site a lot and wondered at what other secrets the world might have to offer. Fortunately, I'd grown out of searching for wild conspiracy theories by the time I was fifteen.

The tutors at university didn't want to see my art go down the gothic route. They were emphatic that they didn't want a rehash of gothic imagery, but I largely ignored them. This was because I was genuinely inspired by these things, and I wasn't going to force myself into doing artwork that didn't inspire me. One of my tutors used to critique my artwork before even asking what it was about. Often his critical remarks would be based on the fact that he thought my work explored certain ideas. Since these not-good-enough ideas were exactly what I had been trying to convey in the first place, I usually ignored him.

I think the tutors' differing opinions wound a lot of you up too, because unlike me, happy to go my own way, many of you would complain about the conflicting advice, confused about which feedback you should take seriously. I only took advice if I thought it was worth taking.

My artwork has matured a lot as I've grown older, and there is less overt horror content to it now. My older paintings often used to be doused in paint made to look like blood or rust, and I was obsessed with creating effects like fog or the crackly feeling of old black and white film. I still like creating the black and white film effect but gone are all the bones and blood and the in-your-face horror. I often work in black ink these days, partly because I had been living in a rented house and didn't want to get oil paint everywhere. Some of my favourite work has been done in ink and dip pen.

At university I was very exuberant and convinced I was going to be a famous artist one day (by the age of twenty-five at the latest, I thought, which felt a very long way off). How I behaved seemed to matter very little at the time, because I just assumed I'd automatically be allowed to be an eccentric if I became a famous artist. I envisioned that I'd be selling my paintings for millions, and that I'd be a new Dalí or Giger. I didn't realise what an elitist club the art world actually is, and that even if I became rich I'd most likely never become part of the club.

These days I am still making artwork, and still trying to innovate and communicate with my audience, but I no longer desire to become a prominent figure in the art world. I decided I had no taste for being seen as a curiosity, or for playing the part of the Satanic artist who amuses the rich. At the time I was not a social butterfly and would have been nervous about meeting new people, especially at social events. Because of the schizophrenia, I have little motivation to be continually producing artwork, and I strongly suspect that the stress of living my life as a high-profile figure would make me ill. My health is more important to me now, after all I've been through.

Schizophrenic symptoms are broken into two camps, what psychologists term positive and negative symptoms. This makes them sound as though they are good and bad, which is misleading, and I prefer to call them active and passive symptoms. The active (positive) symptoms are things like delusions, and hallucinations, whereas the passive (negative) ones are things like blank expressions, monotone speech, lack of interest in the world, and lack of motivation, amongst others.

The lack of motivation I mention especially because it plagues me. The medication I take has an effect on the active symptoms, but unfortunately not on the passive ones. I often have to remind myself of this, because on occasions when I can't do anything due to the apathy and lethargy, I feel as if I'm being lazy and not trying hard enough. For me, the lack of motivation is the hardest passive symptom to cope with, and overall comes a close second to the psychotic symptoms of delusions and hallucinations. It is this lack that makes it hard to maintain a job even though I do have one, it's often a struggle to motivate myself. Even to me this sounds lazy, but you must realise that this symptom also makes simple tasks hard. There were times when I couldn't even motivate myself to take a shower or get out of bed, though I am now able to force myself a bit more. I also can only produce artwork when I have the inspiration and the motivation, so cracking the art world would be difficult for me.

I feel sad that all the medications have only been tailored to tackle the active symptoms, because ridding myself of the passive ones would be very useful. The sadness at this thought comes from the fact that the medication is only designed to rid the sufferer of the symptoms that make them behave deviantly, as if society only cares about a person's mental health symptoms if they are causing a nuisance to others.

I think that schizophrenia and other psychoses are in a different category to most mental health disorders because they involve a break from reality. Many other disorders do not have this feature, OCD, for example, may be torment for those suffering it. Sufferers may feel mad, but their illness doesn't distance them from the real. Not that I want to further stigmatise schizophrenia, because I am well aware that living in a delusional state isn't the fault of the sufferer.

Sadly, schizophrenia and other conditions which cause psychosis are the diagnoses that make people afraid of mental illness. Psychoses make the sufferer act bizarrely, and thanks to the news media playing up the stereotype of the dangerous psychotic, the thing that most people know about schizophrenia is that it can cause people to behave dangerously. These instances of dangerous behaviour are rare, I would like to emphasise. Empathy is a more appropriate response than fear.

There is also a strange disconnect amongst people when they think of mental illness. It's a feeling that isn't usually there with physical illness. People are afraid of mental illness because they fear becoming ill themselves, but they also tend to feel it will never happen to them, so the mentally ill are always 'them' rather than 'us'. Even while I was getting ill, I believed I was too stable to ever suffer from a mental illness. Whether this was in part the bravado brought on by my worsening mental health condition or just my general belief, I can't say. I was obviously very wrong.

There has long been a debate on the link between creativity and madness. Dalí was deemed mad by some, but I think he was just eccentric. He seemed to be too productive to be suffering from madness. Perhaps he was on the cusp of it, but he was certainly not psychotic, or suffering the way I suffered.

Where mental ill health and creativity are concerned, I think the link is a hard one to quantify. While I am a creative person, and also a mentally ill person, there were plenty of people on the course with me who were creative and did not become mentally unwell. They were more productive than me because they didn't have to face a constant struggle with the torments of their own minds. But if we put the issue of productivity to the side, then I'd suggest there could be a link between mental illness and creativity. Altered mental states often help the sufferer see things in another way and make connections and patterns that other people wouldn't see. There is also the uninhibited state of the mentally ill to consider, which dispels the fear of exploring wild ideas in the creative process, whether or not these bear fruit.

Another question fundamental to the relationship between creativity and insanity is that of how to define madness. Insanity is something which is often defined by social norms, and therefore also by temporal norms. In most western cultures, cutting oneself is considered part of a mental disorder, whereas in other cultures self-mutilation can be a spiritual act. Accept this and it's not difficult to see that today's madness could become tomorrow's genius.

There are so many creative figures who are mentally ill. The comedian Stephen Fry, for example, Van Gogh, Emilie Autumn, the musician who sings about her fight with bipolar, mathematician John Nash, who suffered with schizophrenia and won a Nobel prize in economics, memorably portrayed by Russell Crowe in the movie A Beautiful Mind. These people and many others show that disabled people do have something special to give to society, whether their unique experiences actively cause them to be creative, or whether their suffering gives them something to draw upon creatively.

After I was ill, many a mental health professional said to me, “We don’t call it schizophrenia, we say you suffered with psychosis.” To me this was stupid, because I found that having a label empowered me. It got me the help I needed and helped me to understand that I wasn’t alone. It’s inaccurate too, because psychosis is distinct from schizophrenia. Schizophrenia causes psychosis, but psychosis can be a feature of many illnesses, from bipolar to post traumatic stress syndrome. There’s even post-partum psychosis.

The label of psychosis in place of schizophrenia is often inaccurate. Some people have one psychotic episode and that’s all, in which case psychosis is the right term for it. However, my lingering symptoms, and my diagnosis of paranoid schizophrenia, suggests that referring to schizophrenia as psychosis is the wrong thing to do.

The idea behind the name change is to stop stigma. But the decision to avoid the term schizophrenia reinforces stigma instead of fighting it. I feel it is up to the patient to use whichever term they feel most comfortable with. Some people hate a label, whereas others are happy to be labelled. We label everything anyway, from birds to flowers to trees. We don’t agonise over labelling a physical illness: we call a cold a cold, and happily say that cystic fibrosis is cystic fibrosis. So, to me schizophrenia is still schizophrenia. It is attitudes that need to change, not words.

But I digress. Despite meeting you, my fellow art students, I feel as though I learned very little of value from university. I learned something, yes, but I learned more from becoming ill. My illness confronted me with so many aspects of myself and the world which would otherwise have remained hidden, because they were such uncomfortable and even painful realities.

Letter to the voices: Part Three
Storthes Hall
Sept 2006-Oct 2006

Wheel of Fortune

Rage ... Elation... Despair.
These emotions, these the unholy trinity,
were the three emotions within me.

Not Anger... happiness... or sadness.
With this illness they were magnified.
Like a wafer-thin piece of me pressed on a slide.
Like a piece of me that died.

Which emotion will come through next?
Will it be rage? Causing me to smash up the room,
which was my cage... my prison.

Perhaps it will be elation,
the moment the voices said something I liked.
"Look at her, she must be Satan."
A fantasy of my own creation.

Will it be despair? That black feeling,
lower than sadness, darker than guilt.
I lie here on the blackness of my quilt and try shut them out.

Waiting for rage to take me again.

After my deceptions during the previous year, I began my second year at Storthes Hall feeling oddly okay about living there. Generally staying at Storthes into your second year was considered a loser thing to do, because most people had made friends by that point, and moved into shared houses with their companions. I had very few friendships, though, and certainly none which lasted to the point of getting house shares.

My new room was on the second storey of a four-storey block, and I didn't like where it was situated because I was frightened that people would see into my room from the higher-up flats in the buildings which surrounded it. But my fears didn't stop me from furnishing my room with the usual red light and HELL HERE window sign.

This was the year, the one where you tore me down horribly.

The first I heard from you was a continuation of the rumour you'd been discussing the previous year, except that this time your voices seemed to be the new first-year students living on campus all around me. My delusion at this time, was that the people from my year must have spread the rumour to the new first-years.

As you continued your pretence of being students, I would hear you debating all the time, well into the late hours of the evening. Your debate centred on me, and on whether Satan was real. Was it possible I could conjure demons? Was the demon another manifestation of myself? Was I Satan incarnate? Or was I the Antichrist? I felt excited and energised by these rumours, even though some of you voiced doubts. These were voices I thought of as the non-believers.

"Perhaps it was another student wearing a mask you saw?", they said. "Maybe you were seeing shadows." "Perhaps she just wanks all of the time."

Of all these suggestions, the last one gained traction and hit home the most. I was livid about the suggestion that I masturbated all the time because it made me feel human, as if I was mortal. I wanted people to be afraid of me, not to see me as laughable! When this was suggested you always cruelly laughed. I couldn't take the laughter, and it pained me that people thought of me as comical or ridiculous.

You made it seem as though you thought of me as dirty too, as if I did nothing else with my time, and the laughter was so cruel. It was the kind of laughter I term a minor key titter, the sort which comes when you know someone is talking harshly about you, mocking you. You mocked me, and it angered me. It also hurt.

However, I couldn't tear myself away from your conversations. I felt compelled to listen to you, and your incessant chatter added to my usual sleeping difficulties, making it impossible for me to get any rest. Why did I feel so compelled to know what you were saying? I was desperate to hear the believing ones amongst you say something I wanted to hear. When this happened, it meant the difference between feeling good and bad, the difference between being excited, ecstatic and elated, or between being disgusted, despairing and depressed.

This was not my usual behaviour, when I was well. But these traits of eavesdropping were caused by a combination of factors. Though mostly by the overly intense emotions I felt. I could become completely emotionally exaggerated, even aroused when you said things I liked to hear. But the dark side was that you could also say things I hated. The darkest part was that even if I had tried, I'd have been unable to shut you out.

You always sounded to me as if I could hear you from a long way away, as if you really were occupying another flat on campus and watching me. Your voices sounded faint most of the time, and this made me listen intently to catch what you were saying. The only time your voices sounded louder was when you shouted at my window, "WANKER!" or you spoke directly to me. Most of the time you seemed to talk about me amongst yourselves, which trapped me in a web of emotions, listening to you. The frequent faintness of your voices enhanced the validity of my delusion, because sometimes I'd mishear what you had said, which made you feel real. Later in my illness this caused confusion, because you'd laugh at me for mishearing things you'd said, and then you laughed at me for reacting in the wrong way.

It is very hard to convey how you made me feel in the weeks that followed, I was tired all the time due to not sleeping much, which compounded my problems. There was a constant chatter in my head as you'd talk about me and argue amongst yourselves. You never left me at all, and it wore me down.

"I'm telling you she's evil!" ….and I would feel intense excitement.

"Don't be ridiculous, demons don't exist!" … I'd feel despairing.

"She's just a wanker, the red light being on means she's wanking." ... I felt livid and dirty.

"I'm telling you I saw her with the devil." ...elation.

"She wants you to think that, it's a trick." ...rage.

For weeks you'd elaborate on your theories, day and night, and my emotions would change in accordance with what you'd said, in tight little cycles, that now seem to me reminiscent of the feelings that come with bipolar disorder, except the change of emotions happened faster than I imagine they do in bipolar.

These were not regular emotions. The emotions I felt connected with what you said about me were terribly intense. I describe them to people as being ten times stronger than normal emotions, though of course I have no direct way of measuring.

The constant debate about whether I was a supernatural being or merely an idiot caused me to do one thing that real people did notice, and it involved me falling foul of the internet. You were with me all the way, inside my head, on that day.

On the day in question, I went to the flat of one of the few friends I'd managed to keep, and I found her at her desk browsing a site called The Student Room. This was a site where students could share information about topics like course notes, and which tutors they preferred, or information about Storthes Hall being a former mental institution. At the time I hadn't come across social media, so I quite innocently asked my friend what she was looking at. She told me it was a place where students discussed things.

I wish I could blame you directly for making me suggest my friend set up a post about me, but you never cajoled me into doing such a thing. The only way I could honestly blame you is to say that I was trying to get people to discuss the rumours I'd heard you talking about. I believed you would go ahead and post your thoughts, because you were clearly—as I thought—students yourselves. It never crossed my mind to wonder that I could hear you from so far away, or to question why you'd always discuss me alone and not others.

My friend and I created a thread we entitled Scary Mary, and we made a couple of posts to get it going. After I'd gone back to my flat and had time to think, I realised what a stupid thing I'd done. The magnitude of my mistake hit me, and I decided that I wouldn't go back and look at the Scary Mary thread. But my resolve cracked when my friend, who'd been getting backlash for starting the post, told people I'd been involved. She called me while I was in my flat to tell me some girl was calling me an attention seeker in the replies.

I panicked about this revelation and suggested another stupid thing. I asked my friend to take the blame for starting the thread. She dutifully wrote what I told her to, but my thinking was so scrambled and incoherent as I told her what to say that I think she only made the adjustments to the post because she knew it wouldn't be believed. In the end, I decided I had to go to her flat and face the damage.

I was callous to make her take the blame. I can only imagine that I overreacted to being called an attention seeker, which is a phrase I dislike intensely. The phrase attention seeker is often used to delegitimise people and to invalidate their experiences. It is often bandied around when a person cannot be bothered to understand someone else's life. It is a glib phrase which reduces complex motivations and behaviours to something ridiculous and bland.

I didn't want to be viewed that way, and I panicked.

Now I'd made the thread I couldn't do much about it. My friend offered to delete the post, but I thought that this would be a complicated matter, so I told her not to bother. Of course, had I not been suffering delusions, I'd have never done such a thing in the first place.

When I looked at the thread I was confused by the responses, because none of them aligned with what you were saying about me. There were posts saying I was a freak, or an attention seeker, and posts defending my right to dress and act differently. One person quite fairly said, "So what? Everybody wonders what people are saying about them from time to time."

Some people were very good about it, whereas others were very aggressive, and the cruelty of some people upset me. But nothing I saw was in any way like the rumours I'd been hearing from you. This thoroughly confused me, as I'd felt sure you would have posted your thoughts.

It was right after this incident that you started calling me an attention seeker, adding this most hated phrase to your other insults and torments. Now I believed you were students who'd seen the post.

"Did you hear what she did? I told you she's seeking attention."

"Maybe she was trying to find out who we were, so she could take revenge upon us for what we saw."

"It was just shadows."

"Attention-seeking whore."

On and on you'd go, day by day, never ceasing your debates.

Another attack from you came when you began saying I was suicidal, which at the time was not true. This rumour annoyed me greatly, because once again it implied that I was merely human. I did not like being thought of as human. To me, mankind was a weak species, and everything I was doing was about taking away my humanity and distancing myself from the human condition. The problem is, when you portray yourself as a monster, people start treating you like one.

Around this time, I started exhibiting what psychologists term writing behaviour, which is a symptom of schizophrenia that compels the sufferer to write things down. So, under the glow of my red light and with my curtains open, I'd sit and write. I wrote about what I believed was happening. I wrote whilst all around me I could hear your cries of, "She's writing suicide notes" or alternatively, "No, she's pretending to write suicide notes for attention." There was a constant battle of wills between you. Some of you wanted to defend what I was doing, whereas others wanted to take me down.

I'd write in my books for hours about what I thought was going on, feeling all the time that I was being bullied. Then one evening, as I was writing, I saw a camera flash. A light flashed brightly and momentarily in my room, and I knew via the force of delusion that you had taken a picture of me. I didn't realise that the flash of light was one of your visual tricks, a hallucination, so I believed that students from another flat had taken a 'photo'.

Then I heard your laughter. How was it that you thought you'd got a picture of me masturbating? It must have been the way I was sitting, with my legs hunched up and a book on my lap. The movement of my hand, guiding the pen across the page, must have looked to you as though I was masturbating. You were mistaken, of course, misled by the distance from which you were watching, and by the difficulty of seeing clearly when my red light must have been distorting what you could see. You were wrong, but I was still angry and disgusted by your insinuation.

It was obvious to me that the red light was the cause of the misunderstanding, but pride stopped me switching on the main light. If I changed my behaviour, it would mean you had won, and that I was fallible and human. So the red light remained on.

The constant laughter I had to endure, and the cruelty of your words, together with the apparent evidence of your photograph, made me feel sick. I didn't want people thinking they had a picture of me doing something private, and I didn't want them sharing it with the other students.

I felt I hadn't a friend in the world, yet you persisted with your cruelty. "WANKER!" you'd yell at my window. I was extremely embarrassed by the photographic evidence I thought you had. I could hear you discussing it with what I thought were the other students, but they were just voices too. I know that I acted wrongly, but did you really have to do this to me? I hated you and your constant laughter. You made me think that people believed I was dirty and talentless.

"The dirty bitch."

"She is fucked up."

"Look what we caught her doing, ha ha!"

The next trick you played on me was thought insertion. This is a symptom of schizophrenia which makes random ideas occur to the sufferer, and they feel as if they had always been there. It wasn't until after I was medicated that I realised there were thoughts in my head which had come out of nowhere.

This first happened a few days after the photograph incident. For those few days I heard laughter, and I heard the photo being discussed in detail, the rumour seeming to spread around the university. One Sunday morning I was in my room when, from beyond the window, I heard a crow cawing. Suddenly the thought dropped into my mind that you must have thought I'd made the sound, and that I'd made it during the height of orgasm. Illogical though this may seem now, at the time there was a strange sense to it. I believed you thought this because of the noise music I'd played at the end of the previous university year.

This thought hadn't been in my head before, and now it was there. It seems so odd to me now that I couldn't recognise it as a completely alien idea.

I paced around my room muttering to myself that I'd shot myself in the foot by trying to deceive you the previous year. This went strangely unnoticed by you. Though you were in my head the whole time and knew everything about me, you often pretended to be fallible. Sometimes things escaped your notice, and sometimes you got things totally wrong about me. That was your deception. After all, we were playing games. But as a deceiver I didn't ever expect to become the deceived.

The upshot of the thought insertion was that now, every time the crows cawed, you'd laugh and call me a dirty bitch and a wanker. "Calm down, you daft bitch!"

A similar thing happened at night when the owls hooted. You would joke that I was masturbating all the time, and even though you were part of me, you seemed unaware that this was not the truth.

It was around this time that I identified two different camps for your voices. To me there were the five main ones, who would debate the rumours and spread them around, and then there were the rest of you who represented the other students, the people who heard the rumours and believed them. Because the latter seemed like gullible idiots, my desire not to be human increased, in tandem with my disgust at the human species.

Of the main five voices, your hierarchy seemed to be that the three meanest of you were at the top, whilst the remaining two seemed to debate in my favour. The dominant voice amongst you seemed to be male and incredibly spiteful, while the second in command was a female voice, who was also very nasty. Even now I am haunted by her cruel laugh.

The third in command was another male, who could be swayed either against me or for me depending on the evidence given. The remaining two were nice voices, a male and a female. They would say the things I liked to hear. The female voice sometimes doubted me, but mostly said nice things. The remaining voice was determined to defend all that I did and raised me up on a pedestal.

Later when I was medicated but still very ill, I doubted the intentions of the nicer two. Were you all merely working together, some of you raising me on high so I could continue to fall, giving me hope so that it could be snatched away from me? This seemed like the way to utterly destroy a person.

The nicer of your voices, the ones who believed in my world, were not considered to be gullible fools, even though you believed me without question. The label gullible fools was reserved only for the voices who believed in the rumours I did not enjoy. I was a hypocrite.

The debates among you were often about the rumours you were spreading, and you'd fight for dominance amongst yourselves. I was caught in the middle of this anarchy, unable to escape. The nicer voices deified me which caused me to feel powerful, supernatural and godlike, then the nasty ones tore me down and reduced me to being human. During my experience of schizophrenia, I couldn't piece the facts together, but long afterwards I realised the whole point of your torture was to confront me with the idea I am human. Everything you did was to hammer home this point. You seemed so determined to tear me away from the world in my head and reduce me to being like those I hated. Why did my world offend you so much?

The constant stress of hearing you argue, and the laughter when the owls and crows sounded, made me determined to prove to you that I wasn't worthless. So I started singing a lot in my flat, which was something you all agreed I was good at, and I would go outside and perform gymnastics and taekwondo moves as a way of showing you I could do other things, and that you were wrong about me. This had next to no effect. While I was doing gymnastics you'd shout and make owl noises at me, which made me livid. I felt that you were making these noises to distract me, which made me even more angry, because I worried I'd have an accident due to being antagonised.

One night, my friend Kris invited me to the on-site bar at Storthes Hall, which back then was called D Bar. This bar was only ever full on special occasions, most of the décor was brown and a bit dingy. On this occasion it was very full. I immediately heard laughter. I could only bear to spend five minutes in there with Kris, because I could hear what I thought were people making owl and crow sounds at me. I became extremely upset and told Kris I was leaving the bar because I was depressed but didn't tell him why. I trudged, unhappy, back to my flat.

A Letter to Andy
Doncaster
1993-Present

Out of my Tree

I've got to keep this poem short,
as I cling to the branches of this tree,
his voice like an intrusive thought,
as he sits here next to me.

In my mind I imagined, that I would let go,
but clung on tightly, to his strife,
and his enduring woe.

I stayed up there in my leafy domain,
clinging to the branches of this tree,
the voice that once drove me insane,
as he sits here next to me.

My original idea for a book about my life and illness was based on a series of questions asked by my friends. I'd planned to answer their questions in book form. Andy, your question to me was, "How have your views on religion and faith changed over the years? And what if any influence do they have on you now?"

Even though the book has evolved beyond the Q&A format, I would still like to answer your question. I'm starting my answer from the age of six, because I can't remember what I thought about faith before then.

Long before we met and became friends in sixth form, before I was even in secondary school, I used to be a Christian. I was afraid of the corrupting powers of devils and demons. The notion of monsters who could turn a person away from God was truly scary to me.

Back then I liked to climb the pear tree in my mum's back garden, and often when I did, I'd hear Satan telling me to let go of the branch to which I clung. He had a sneering voice like a villain from a children's show. Fortunately, his voice was inside my head, not outside my head as the voices later were. My experience in the pear tree was more like an intrusive thought than a hallucination and its accompanying delusion.

It is worth mentioning the external nature of the voices to you to help you understand. Though I sometimes refer to the voices in my head, the voices never seemed to come from inside my head. In fact they did not sound like an internal voice at all, but as if an external voice was talking to me. I could hear them from different directions, and in different tones, at different volumes, and none of them were my own voice, or even the voice of anyone I knew. In this I was unlike some people with schizophrenia, who hear voices of people they know.

When I was young, I attended a Christian group called Girls' Brigade, and was very enthusiastic about it, especially about the singing. One year when I was about ten, and Girls' Brigade had broken up for the summer, I was lying on my bed, on the top bunk, thinking about the universe, when suddenly a thought came upon me. What if all the things they taught at Girls' Brigade were not true? What if there was no God?

I scared myself terribly with this thought and felt guilty for thinking it. I tried to squash the idea, but it had taken hold, and I kept questioning it. Soon afterwards I decided to leave Girls' Brigade, but for an unrelated reason. The reason I left was that we as a group had to collectively pick what modules we were going to study for the next term. I wanted to do animal care, but the rest of the girls vetoed me and chose the childcare module, in which I had very little interest. I tried to stick it out but found myself so bored with it; we were basically learning how to sterilise milk and look after dolls. I had little interest in the raising of children. So I left, but leaving a group who believed in God probably did not help me with my doubts.

As I got older, around age twelve, I started taking an interest in science and astrophysics, and began to embrace the idea of a scientific world. Astrophysics still gave me the scope to wonder about the nature of God and why the universe is here, which is why I enjoyed the subject so much. I felt that the universe was a huge and mysterious place, and that studying astrophysics gave me reason to believe. But it also gave me many other options and possibilities, such as whether there really is nothing, whether there is a God, or a pantheon of gods. Or even a God and no afterlife, or an afterlife but no God.

One of my favourite books around this time was called One Hundred Things We Don't Know About Science (and no one else does either). I loved that book because although I have a scientific mind, I also love the mystery of not knowing. I loved that there were questions unanswered, a reason to see that we don't know it all and that there could be other answers, whether scientific or in theology. Some of the questions in this book have probably been answered now, but the bigger universe-centric questions probably have not.

As I became a teenager, I started becoming religious again, and started exploring Wicca and Paganism. But all the books I read on the subject at the time disappointed me, perhaps because they were mainstream, made-for-the-market books aimed at young teenagers. Even the look of these books put me off. They all had glossy covers featuring fantasy art or photographs, whereas I wanted dusty old mysterious books. They also had spells in them that I considered banal, like spells to attract a boyfriend (I had no interest in anyone at the time), spells to find a lost object (I'd just look for the lost object), spells to help and heal people, and spells to purify the home. These spells seemed to be things that could be achieved anyway, without the need for rituals, as fun as they may be. I also had difficulty believing that burning herbs and chanting words would achieve the ends I desired.

These days I appreciate that there is a bit more to pagan beliefs than just spells. But as fun as all the trappings of witchcraft are, I believe that if spells really do work, that it is the force of will which achieves the results. If there is indeed really a spirit world, a world of magic, then the very fact that you want to contact it should be enough. No amount of candles, words, herbs, and phases of the moon are more powerful than desire.

Don't get me wrong, when I was performing rituals I liked to use things like candles, words, and tomes. But I appreciated them more for their ability to enhance the feel of the ritual, not because I believed they did anything special. All the trappings of witchcraft are created by humans, including the dreaded Ouija board. They might be good tools for demonstrating that you want to touch the spirit world, but I'm certain there is no actual magic in them.

I was never a big believer in astrology either, which is often popular in witchcraft circles. I failed to see how the movements of the planets amongst the stars could have any effect on the daily lives of humans. I could also not get on with the idea that all people with the same sign would have the same month. But despite my lack of faith in the trappings of witchcraft, I did obtain a fair few objects, mostly to show my fellow students that I'd chosen this path.

I didn't stick with Wicca for long, though, because I wanted something darker. The idea of black magic always made more sense to me than white. The reason I say this is because with white magic, the results often don't require the use of magic at all. With black magic, you're doing things that you wouldn't get away with so easily in polite society. It is easier to hex someone than to punch them in the face in terms of avoiding getting yourself into trouble. Black magic, for me, was a kind of cowardly way of getting what I needed. Even if there is no spirit world, and no one heard my desires, I could at least feel like I'd acted. It's almost the same as hitting the angry face icon on Facebook.

My quest for darkness led me to Voodoo, but having being raised in a monotheistic society I had trouble adapting my mindset to the pantheon of gods—called Loas—in Voodoo magic. There was probably a lot more I didn't grasp about this religion. I found out that Voodoo uses a mixture of white and black magical workings, and some of the books I read were extremely interesting. It was the scary media-driven image of Voodoo that attracted me, but I discovered a complex and fascinating set of beliefs and practices.

I first got into Satanism at the age of fifteen, when a boy in design and technology class at school asked me why I was wearing the star of the Antichrist. It was actually a pentagram on my hooded top, a pagan symbol, and the top was just one I happened to like. I thought nothing of the boy's comment until the bell rang to signal the end of the lesson. As I walked down the corridor, I felt strangely proud that the boy had conflated me with evil, and the idea came upon me that I wanted to worship Satan.

It was two years after this that I discovered modern Satanism and Anton LaVey's Church of Satan.

I do feel I owe the Church of Satan something, even though

my discovery of it made me feel very conflicted. LaVey's work gave my practice some direction and steered me away from becoming an actual monster in my pursuit of evil.

As I mentioned before, LaVey's Satanism is atheistic. Although I loved the logic and sense to his writings—and his use of psychology—I felt I didn't quite fit in with his outlook. This caused me a lot of internal conflict because I wanted to be in accord with LaVey, but I also wanted the kind of beliefs offered by the Christian church. I wanted to believe what LaVey said because I respected his mind, but I wanted to believe what Christians believed because this meant an opportunity to be evil.

I liken my fascination with an evil Satan as being akin to those people who are obsessed with serial killers. It is an attraction towards the darkness in someone else, rather than being a bad person myself. However, I was uninterested in mortal evils, perhaps feeling they were too close to home. The evil characters I liked in cinema were all supernatural themed bad guys, and seemed less gritty than, say, a gangster-type bad guy.

These days I realise life is not as simple as pure good and evil, life is a lot more varied and colourful than that.

Back in school, when I pretended a sincere belief in Christianity, I wanted people to see me as dark and totally sure of myself, even though I had a strong agnostic streak. Like any other religion, Satanism has a disrespect for any other groups or offshoots from the main theology. LaVeyans claim that theistic Satanists are not doing the right thing, and the theistic side say the same of the LaVeyans. This is the ugly side of religion, when we tell each other we are doing the wrong thing if we do it differently. This dogmatic approach caused me to feel conflicted, because I didn't want someone telling me I was doing things wrong and taking my agency away from me.

I didn't do much to dispel the media myths around modern Satanism, and in part it was because of the media imagery that I wanted to appear so sure of myself. In movies and books Satanists are absolutely sure of themselves. They conjure demons and do dark acts. In reality Satanists are rarely as portrayed in the movies, living normal lives and having ordinary jobs and hobbies. Terry Pratchett and Neil Gaiman's book Good Omens is an excellent representation of the normality of life as a Satanist, but in school I feared being laughed at if I told the truth. I have experienced many things that could be said to be supernatural occurrences. But I wasn't always sure that they were supernatural, or whether they were purely scientific, related to my mental health condition or plain coincidence. So, despite having had out of body experiences, visions I can't explain, and a suspicion that I sometimes I predict things, I also see that there could be a rational explanation.

These days I still have beliefs but I no longer place then under the banner of Satanism. My beliefs as they stand are quite vague, I believe in some sort of afterlife but I admit I do not know what that entails. I certainly don't think of the afterlife as a realm of pure happiness. My preferred vision is that it's a progression, we are three dimensional beings in this universe but then we move on to being four dimensional and living in that sphere. Of course I do not know if there is any truth to this.

I have vague ideas that we are not here by accident but can't determine why we would be here.

I have discovered, through my fascination with both science and theology, that every idea people have regarding the universe is met with what I term 'The Infinity Problem', in which every theory people hold ends up having infinity as its end point. If a person believes in God, then God has been there infinitely. When regarding the big bang, one must consider what came before it, and before that.

Some people believe the universe is a simulation, but then must ask who created our universe simulation, and whether the creator's universe is also a simulation. There are many other examples I could give. This infinity end point has always fascinated me, because it is a conundrum. I remember when you yourself were talking about God in school, asking me at what point in infinity did God decide to create the earth. This is a very interesting philosophical question.

As I said before, at school I always hid my agnostic streak, and even today I am still exploring the mysteries of religion, trying to decide what I believe. One thing that did prompt me to hide my doubts was the justification of myself, specifically the question of how I'd justify myself as an agnostic Satanist to others, particularly since I'm not a bad person. This was difficult to get my head around because I thought that, if Satan does exist and is the Christian antagonist how can I understand my motivations for being this way? If I show support for an evil being does this not make me complicit in all the things he's said to do?

If I was atheistic, LaVeyan Satanism would have suited me quite well. But I'm simultaneously blessed and cursed with agnosticism, which in some ways does overcomplicate matters of religion. Especially as I saw myself as a Satanist, a Christian (for example) who might be doubtful can still justify their actions, because they are not exploring their darknesses or that which is considered to be bad.

One thing I can say motivated me is compassion. I saw so much of Satan in myself, and in my own behaviours, even down to the way the general population viewed me. I found it far easier to relate to a flawed Satan than an abstract God.

Something about the religion of Satanism that seems to scare people is the word ritual. The phrase 'Satanic ritual' seems to provoke an especially strong reaction. But our lives are full of rituals and rites. Going to church on Sunday is a ritual, and getting married is full of little rituals, such as at the altar, the first dance, the cutting of the cake, and the speeches. There's nothing inherently evil about a ritualistic approach. Of course I never said this to anyone at the time because my image largely played upon peoples' ignorance or lack of knowledge.

In the early days of my practice I didn't perform rituals. I felt under-confident about performing them, and living at home with my mum wasn't the most ritual-friendly setting. At the time these inhibitions did make me feel inadequate, since I wanted to be seen as evil, and ritual is the scariest part to outsiders.

When I found the confidence to perform Satanic rituals, I quickly grew to enjoy the sense of fantasy and purpose they gave me. Nowadays my shrine collects dust in the corner. I've still not been able to bear deconstructing it, because losing a religion is quite a difficult matter.

It was around the time of getting into Satanism that I became interested in spiritual corruption, of the sort where good becomes evil. I think this fascination influenced the path I chose, because it was then that I realised I enjoyed the idea of becoming evil. This is why the Judeo-Christian vision of the fall of Lucifer interested me so much.

I have always been interested in change and transformation. This is obvious when I look back at the toys I played with, and the things I liked as a child. I enjoyed the scene from Fantasia about the forming of the world and evolution of the dinosaurs. I liked Power Rangers, Pokémon, Animorphs and Beast Wars. All these things involved evolution or transformation of some kind. So, it was my fascination with transformation which turned into the desire to be corrupted, and I loved scenes like the one in Star Wars where Luke is tempted to join the dark side. In my case, I fully intended to fall. I was hooked on that pivotal moment when the tempted fails to resist.

The irony of me, having had my Satanic preoccupations, then suffering with paranoid schizophrenia does not escape me. This is an illness which shows me visions and makes me hear voices, and is very much like a textbook portrayal of demonic possession.

My way of viewing the world has, as you can see, caused me great chagrin. But even while I wished to be more certain of myself, I also knew that having doubts, and being slower to believe, was a kind of strength. It's a strength which makes it possible to critically examine any information I am given, and to see other possibilities. It makes me who I am today.

A Letter to Al
Storthes Hall
Nov 2005- Mar 2006

Community Church

I was only playing mind games, what could possibly go wrong?
You wanted me to come to church, so I thought I'd go along.
You oh ardent Christian, and me dressed so Satanic.
When you first invited me, I said 'No thanks' and I'd panicked.
I wanted you to know that there was no changing me.
So I came along to prove to you, that a leopard doesn't change its tree…
Or is that spots?...or ideals?...or punchlines?
So I dressed up in my Gothic attire.
Hoping to smite them with my ungodly fire.
I was planning to startle them with my iniquity and vice.
But would you bloody have guessed it? Turns out they were nice.
Though I did not enjoy the sermons and avoided all the songs.
Though they were determined to straighten out my wrongs...
Or was that save me?… Or change me?….. Or befriend me!
The one thing that really struck me, was their sense of community.
And though I haven't changed my 'tree.'
And still behave Satanically.
I made a few new friends.
And that's all that matters in the end.

Firstly, I must say sorry. I'm sorry for the way I treated you and your faith. I was completely horrible, and I hadn't set out with the intent of treating you the way I did. I was simply trying to protect myself and my own fragile identity, and as a result behaved very cruelly to you.

While at Storthes, and while ill, I was very conflicted. Sometimes I hated being around people, and yet at other times I craved company. This is why our first real meeting was in the TV lounge. I often went there, not to watch the TV, but to read, television being too human a pursuit. Usually I'd be left to my own devices while I was in there, but what else could I expect when I made sure people stayed away from me?

On the occasion of our meeting, I was in the TV lounge reading and I noticed a group come into the corridor. I didn't realise at first that they were from the Christian Union. They were all chattering, and I can't remember how, but they got talking to me. This conversation ended with me showing the group some gymnastics moves, and when I stood up after performing them, I spotted you and our eyes met. You gave me a gentle smile.

Your group soon moved on. You were, I think, the last to arrive, and you all left for your Christian Union meeting. I gave little thought to our encounter, and after you had gone I continued to read my book. I wasn't really looking for a partner at the time, considering myself to be non-human and above such matters, and so I was surprised when you came to find me again. You and your friend were planning to watch the new Batman Begins DVD in your room, and you asked me to join you. I decided to accept your invitation because I was lonely.

I can't remember all the times we met up, nor do I recall most of the nicer things we did together. The more dramatic of our encounters have stuck firmly in my mind though. On one occasion we were in your flat, and I spotted the Bible that was customary in every room. There was even one in my room, and I hadn't destroyed or defaced it. I pointed to your bible and said, "Why do they provide a Bible with the room? Surely a Christian would have one anyway?"

Then you looked at me in a funny way and replied, "I don't know...I forgot mine."

"You're a Christian?" I said, slightly shocked.

You nodded slightly, and I kept my mouth shut about my beliefs, even though they were no secret.

One of the strange things about schizophrenia is the way the sufferer's memories get distorted. I'd known you'd been with the Christian Union the first time we met, but I had forgotten it. That's the thing with this illness: sometimes I'd be completely oblivious, whereas at other times I'd piece facts together faster than the average person.

Another occasion I recall was once when we were both coming home from somewhere, and you walked me back to my flat. When we entered my room, I put my Satanic Bible back on my lectern. I can't recall why I'd been carrying the book with me, but I placed it back on the stand where I kept it. You asked me quietly, "Are you a Satanist?"

A slight nod from me this time.

"It's really dangerous, what you are into." you told me.

At the time all I could do was reply "You'll find someone else."

It was only at this point that I realised you had romantic intentions towards me. Again, I think I was slow to realise your interest because of my illness causing me to be oblivious.

Around this point in my life, I thought of myself as incapable of loving, and had only let the relationship between us proceed because I knew it couldn't work, not without one of us changing for the other. I also knew that with you being a Christian, you'd not pressure me for sex before I was ready, so I felt safe to let our relationship continue, knowing that I could go out with you without sexual relations being an issue.

It became clear that this compromise wasn't going to work.

Neither of us was going to change, and now I knew you believed my religion to be dangerous things seemed hopeless. But you still spent time with me and called me on the internal landline most nights. I became so accustomed to your calls that one night when you didn't call, I cried bitterly. It was only later I remembered that Thursdays were when your Christian Union meetings were held.

You told me you'd like to teach me about your faith, but that you didn't want to learn about mine. I didn't mind you not wanting to learn about Satanism, because back then I was still very confused and didn't want to break character by having to answer awkward questions about my religion.

The first event you took me to was the Christian Union party, where we played games and had cake and snacks. Despite the fact I had fun at the party, I felt there was something missing. I came to realise that what was lacking was a sense of danger. No alcohol was served that night, and as a result the party felt very much like a child's birthday. Everything about it felt too safe, no one was loud or rowdy, and it all felt like good clean fun. I don't know why this bothered me, because I'm not usually a person who enjoys too much shouting and falling out. I however left the party with the sense that Christianity shields itself from any type of danger, and somehow loses something because of it.

I was extremely surprised that you didn't break relations with me on a later occasion when you found me sitting in the TV lounge with the head of a pheasant. I was telling the truth when I told you I hadn't killed it, but of course I had it on me because I wanted people to think I had killed it, to further convince the other students that I was evil.

Your unfazed response to this incident made me realise that you were drawn to me as your opposite. Christianity lacks darkness and danger, and I think you may have been drawn to me for the very thing your religion could not provide. I recall you telling me how you liked graphically gritty and violent films, which struck me as a contradictory, given your faith. But I notice that good people will often be drawn to darkness, and bad people often like to justify themselves as full of light. I am not exempt from this kind of contradiction, of course. For example, I find kittens cute and amusing.

Despite the sense that our relationship was doomed, we spent some good times together, playing video games and watching anime. Though of course talk of religion would often cause heated debates, with me arguing anyway I could against your beliefs. I found the whole thing surreal, almost funny. We were like a parody of Romeo and Juliet.

Though you were interested in me, I found whenever I tried to reciprocate these feelings you'd clam up, and would seem tense, almost embarrassed, or scared, and I wondered if your coldness in these moments was because you were having an internal struggle with your faith. I knew you liked me, but I started to get the impression that you didn't know what you wanted. Our relationship must have been just as confusing to you as it was to me.

Things probably would have continued in this vein had you not tried to change me. You were determined I should learn first-hand about how caring and good your god is. This was when things started going sour, because I must confess that I started playing mind games with you.

My games started innocently enough. I was determined to prove to you that a person can't be changed if they don't want to be. But then it started to become a sport to me. I'd devise ways to keep you interested in the relationship, by doing things that implied there was hope for change. For instance, I would show you I was making an effort to read the Bible, or I'd playfully don your Christian Union sweater when we were in your flat. The purpose of my game-playing was to prolong your torment rather than to crush your faith. I enjoyed the drama of our heated debates and wanted you to learn the hard way that I could not be changed.

This was entirely the wrong way to handle the situation. Treating you as an avatar in my game was undoubtedly cruel, and I apologise. I regret that I've not apologised to you sooner. Saying sorry about this is hard because I am still in turmoil over things I did.

It was my game-playing that caused me to come along on the Alpha Course, a Christian educational course set up by your church with the aim of teaching non-Christians what Christianity is really about. The course meetings were held in the evenings, and I somehow got it into my head that I should present the other side of the argument, as if it was my duty to do so.

Food was served before the meetings, which kept me turning up each week, because it meant I wouldn't have to cook on Wednesdays. Yes, you fed me, and I kept coming back. It is funny to me now that I thought I was being respectful of your religion by hiding my inverted cross around Christians, because nothing else I did was respectful.

I wouldn't listen, and indeed had no intention of listening. I shouted down the reverend and acted angrily. One night, after a few Wednesdays of my argumentative and cruel behaviour, the reverend, Trevor, offered us both a lift back to Storthes. I knew this was going to be his chance to talk to me about my behaviour. Part of me was excited about the chat, because it meant I'd have a chance to discuss Satanism. The other part of me was nervous at the possibility I'd overstepped the mark.

Another thing that was bothering me about having to go home

in Trevor's car was the fact I didn't smell too good. Hygiene is something that goes out of the window with schizophrenia, and though I did regularly wash, the clothes I wore were not always totally clean, especially my coats, which often had mud on the hem from walking in the woods at night. I do not know why I smelt so bad on that night, but earlier on that evening while I was waiting for you to come to collect me, to walk me to the Alpha Course, I heard someone remark of me "I didn't know humans could make that sort of smell." This could have been my voices, but I was hurt by the remark. I felt even more upset when I realised it was true.

Trevor drove us back to Storthes Hall in silence, along the long, dark, winding roads that were quite usual round Huddersfield. The journey seemed to take forever, and I almost got to the point of thinking that I'd been wrong, and that he was just offering us a lift home. Until, that is, we arrived at the stony frontage of Storthes Hall, and he spoke.

"I take it you're a Satanist?" he said gravely.

I nodded slowly and said defiantly, "Yes."

"How long have you been into this?"

"Since I was thirteen." I was adding my earlier interest in witchcraft on to the figure.

"I think you need to calm down." He said quietly. "And just try and listen to what we have to say."

I didn't reply.

He continued, "Are there a group of you?"

To which I replied with a haughty, "Yes. Back in Doncaster."

This was a complete fabrication, and one of the rare times that I told an outright lie. I told this lie because I wanted you both to know I was serious and wouldn't be easy to extract from my religion. Or at least from my adoration of Satan.

"Perhaps you should come to church and see what it's really about." he said.

Your voice piped up from the back of the car, "Yeah, you could see for yourself. We sing songs too. You like singing."

I replied, "No." But I knew that to continue my games, I'd need to go to church at some point in the future. I knew if I didn't you might lose interest in me. I knew it was futile, that I was just prolonging the slow decline of our relationship, but in my head, I was having too much fun to quit.

So after a few arguments, with me pretending I didn't want to go, I ended up agreeing to come along.

One night in D Bar we met up, and you presented me with a Christmas present. It was a CD of music you had made, and you'd taken the time to draw a digital image of me in my gothic finery as the cover art. I was quite touched. You also invited me to stay at your parents' home over the new year period.

So at the end of that year, I spent a long weekend with you and your family. It was one of the most harmonious times we spent together, and I recall we didn't have too many arguments. I think I was behaving myself while I was being treated with courtesy by your parents.

On seeing your parents' house, I was surprised. It was a terraced house and it looked small on the outside, but inside it seemed enormous. I met your parents and their friends on the first night I stayed over. We celebrated New Year. The fire was roaring, and in my long gothic coat I was too warm. I was particularly impressed with the food. Your mum's slow-roasted parsnip crisps and potato salad with mustard mayonnaise dressing were divine. We played word games with the guests, and I had a good time.

Later in the evening we sat out on your parents' bench round the side of their house and discussed religion. I tried not to be too argumentative, and the conversation was less heated than usual. I enjoyed the rest of that long weekend, which was spent taking walks and meeting your friends at the local pub.

I felt awkward on only one occasion when, after a walk through a muddy field, I had dirtied the hem of one of my long coats. I'd planned to wear the coat the following day, knowing that it was the one you liked most on me. So in the morning I surreptitiously washed the hem in the bathroom sink. I didn't want to get into trouble for doing this, and I was aware I was taking too long in the bathroom. We went to church that day, which made me feel nervous, because I didn't know how people might react to me. It ended up being fine, as your sister also dressed in an alternative style. The reverend didn't seem too perturbed by me, and we had a pleasant conversation which I didn't feel I needed to spoil by being rude.

The only bad night I had during my stay was one night which was marred by a horrible episode of sleep paralysis. I had suffered from this condition throughout my life, waking up paralysed and scared. After this bout, when I was eventually able to move again, I sat in the corridor of your house waiting for you to wake up.

On the day I left I was talking to your mum while hefting my luggage down the stairs. I mentioned that my nickname at home was Hell, and was surprised when she replied, "That's not very nice!"

"My mum calls me it." I answered, confused. I didn't see what the problem was, as it was just a shortening of the name Helen.

Going to your church back in Huddersfield was a strange experience for me. Despite myself I did learn a lot about Christianity, and about the way Christians view the world, even if I only used it as a way of internally critiquing your religion.

The first thing that bothered me about going to church was other people finding out I was going to church. I felt strangely guilty about it, as if I was betraying myself and peoples' notions of me.

But the allure of continuing my game made me decide to go ahead with it. I went along each week, taking the bus and then walking from the town centre out to the church. I didn't really join in much, or enjoy myself when I got there, but stayed silent and was more respectful than I had been on the Alpha course. This time I didn't shout at anyone.

I enjoyed the singing at the beginning of the session more than I enjoyed the sermons. I didn't join in with the singing because the lyrics were not my kind of thing, but I appreciated the music.

Your church was a surprise to me, because every church I'd visited when I was young had been a very sombre affair. My memories of church from childhood were of massive candles, and of thinking that the reverend was God because of his white robes. I asked my mum, "Can I give God some of my Smarties?"

Your church was thoroughly modern. It wasn't just the building but the proceedings which seemed so different to my past experience of church. The people seemed to be very lively, the music was Christian rock, and there was a large participatory element to the proceedings as well.

People could stand up and testify how God had touched their lives.

In spite of these positives, I couldn't get on board with it. I had such a shaky sense of my own beliefs. However, seeing so many people enjoying their faith made me yearn for a group of like-minded people who could support me. Being ill played a big part in my confusion, because the illness made me more prone to believing similar things to Christianity, whereas the other part of me tugged me towards my doubts. I found, and still find today, that faith can be a fluctuating thing. Some days I believe in things more strongly, whereas on other days I am riddled with doubts.

During the sermons I'd sit quiet, but my mind was filled with ideas. I'd debate in my head what Trevor said about the loving nature of God. I recall on one occasion when he likened God to a father, saying that fathers should punish their children when they've done wrong. I immediately thought "Yes, but not for eternity!" Trevor also said that Satan can only do things God allows him to do, and I thought this a massive contradiction to the loving nature of God, almost as if God is merely keeping his hands clean.

The only part of going to church that I wholeheartedly enjoyed was the social at the end, when coffee and tea was served from the kitchen hatch. Despite my dark and brooding manner and odd dress sense I did make a few friends at church. I appreciated the sense of community I felt between them, and it was clear that the congregation looked out for one another. But I was playing games there too.

The reason I kept returning to your church was because I knew people there would take me seriously, and reinforce my notion of myself as evil. I was a sinner amongst the flock.

When I look back it isn't completely clear to me why I was seeking evil so much. When I examine the things I did, I felt like I was being evil or at least very misguided. There is a parallel between my behaviour and the textbook behaviour of demons. I relished peoples' fear and enjoyed sowing discord and sometimes doubt amongst the congregation by probing and questioning what they believed. One friend at the church told me he believed that the two warring kingdoms of heaven and hell would reunite eventually, to which I asked, "Then why does it matter which kingdom I choose?"

I think a lot of my behaviour was about control. I wanted to control the world and how people perceived me. I am not by nature a controlling person, but there was part of me that yearned to be the god of my own little kingdom because the world is such a frightening and turbulent place.

On one occasion Trevor told me off because he thought I was dressing in a deliberately Satanic manner. This upset me because I'd actually attempted to downplay the outfit I wore that day, even though I did have a black veil over my face and a fur stole. I burst into tears and tried to explain myself; laughing or crying with little provocation is a symptom of schizophrenia.

He asked, "Why do you still come here, if you don't enjoy it? I'm starting to think you are up to something sinister." By way of excuse, I pointed in your direction. I could hardly tell him the truth of the matter.

Much later when I told my mum about this incident, she was horrified. "Churches," she said, "should be accepting of people no matter who they are, or what they look like."

When we left the church later that day we argued, and you accused me of being mean-spirited. This set me off crying again, we sat on the bus together in silence. I knew things were coming to an end between us.

The final nail in the coffin between you and me came when I called you on the internal landline in my sleep. I couldn't remember making the call. I'd stood up and gone over to the window. I looked out, and I could see a student burning something on the grass outside my flat. I watched as the fire went out and the student ran away. Soon after that, a knock came at my door. In my paranoia, thinking it was the student I'd seen coming to burn my flat down, I called out, "Who is it?" The reply came that it was the security staff, and when I opened the door, you were there with a female security guard.

I was confused and explained why I hadn't opened the door straight away. You told me that you hadn't seen a student burning things on the way over. I realise now that this was a hallucination.

The security woman said, "You must have had a nightmare."

"I haven't even been to sleep!" I said surprised.

It transpired that I'd rung you up without being aware of it, and that I'd said I'd been drinking vodka and orange, and that I had a headache. You'd thought the caller hadn't sounded like me.

For quite a while afterwards I believed I must have fallen asleep and not known it, and made the call while still sleeping. But now I believe the phone call was not made by me at all. A friend of mine from those days was extremely jealous that I chose to spend time with you instead of her, and I think she may have been the one who made the call to you that night. After all, she always drank vodka and orange, and you thought the caller hadn't sounded like me.

After that incident I saw much less of you, but still I tried to cling to the tatters of what was left. I tried hard to remain your friend, even though our relationship was effectively over. I started to feel very alone around this time, and missed being asked to events by you. This was very much my own fault, of course. I'd had a choice. I could have treated you with more respect.

The last time we spoke at university was when you were on the way to the laundrette. I was sitting on the grass, and as you passed me I said "Hi." We exchanged some brief and awkward words, and then you left. I saw you walking on a different path on your return from the laundrette, which I assumed you did so you could avoid meeting me again.

A Letter to Al: Part Two
Doncaster and Huddersfield
2008-2009

I saw a Demon

We know thus far that I am mad.
I perceive things which are not there,
and sometimes even believe them.
So believe me when I say I saw a demon.
With his coal black skin.
And red halo of light emanating from him.
Atop my bookcase there he sat.
Immovable and dark, with wings folded back.
A vision?
A dream?
A hallucination?
Madness, a pro: you see things.
Madness, a con: no one believes you.

It was a long time before we spoke again, and that was mostly through Facebook. When I first discovered social media, I added a lot of people I knew while I'd been ill and getting ill, partly to let them know I'd been unwell. I hoped they would realise that a lot of my behaviour back then had been due to my failing mental health.

I'll admit I have trouble letting go of past situations and people, so I stayed in touch with you, and every so often I would message to see how you were. I was still visiting Huddersfield, having left university in April 2007, and would still visit the church from time to time. I don't know really what I was doing returning to church. I still had my friends there, and I used the excuse that I wanted to see them. My thinking is that it was habit, a routine that I clung to. I often while at home missed my red-lit room and would lay and strain my ears listening to the voices, who were much fainter at this time. This was habit too. Part of me wanted to go back and relive the torment, because it was familiar.

At this point I was still in the very early stages of recovery, having only being diagnosed and medicated in the April of 2007. I tried to go back to uni for my third year in September 2007, but I only lasted six weeks. I was still too ill to function and was sleeping a lot. I walked round uni during those six weeks convinced that everybody hated me, suffering from residual paranoia. Recovery from schizophrenia is very slow, and it is only when I look back now that I realise how ill I still was at that point.

In 2009 I messaged you on Facebook to say I was thinking about becoming a Christian. And I almost did exactly that, coming very close to getting baptised. Later, after this failed attempt at changing my religion, you asked me why I hadn't followed through with it.

The answer is that around this time I was in shock at what had happened to me, so I convinced myself that becoming a Christian was the way to go, because my illness was scary and had upended my reality. Also, there was the boredom. So much was happening at the time, but it felt like nothing could touch me, as if I was viewing my life through a veil and not taking part in it. I was looking for change, and for something to shake my life up in a good way. It was this boredom that convinced me to go back to university.

But I didn't want to go back to the lonely university life I'd had before. I thought it would be nice to have the sense of community that I saw in Christianity, a group of people I could be friends with, and who would look out for me. Part of me was curious as to whether something could change within me, whether through encountering God I would change. Perhaps I was also having a crisis of faith. So I made arrangements to get baptised at the church in Huddersfield, but at last minute I got cold feet. The day before my baptism, I called up one of my Christian friends and told them I couldn't go ahead with it. At the time you knew about my change of heart, but not the reasons behind it.

My reasons were complex. But ultimately, I was not ready to let go of the identity I had forged all these years. I was inspired by darkness, particularly the darkness within me, and if I became a Christian, I would have been denied the chance to explore this. It seemed to me too that there was no way Christianity could be reconciled with my sexual side. Despite my fear of discussing sexuality, I am swayed by my baser instincts. There is nothing unhealthy about my sexuality, but my fantasy material draws on themes that Christians would consider dangerous.

I also felt I would never be able to meet with God because I would never be able to let go of my dark past. I imagine that if I did become a Christian, I'd be the sort that relished knowing I'd had a murky background, a background which would make me different to those around me. I feel I am not spiritually made for Christianity because of my 'pull towards darkness', a phrase you've heard me use many times to describe my inclination towards Satan. When I first mentioned this, you said it was something you didn't understand, but I suspect it may have been something you just didn't recognise in yourself. After all, I feel you were attracted to me because of my darkness, not despite it.

I attracted many Christian friends while at your church, and I don't necessarily think they were all drawn to me because they felt I needed saving. It was more that I represented something different, a darkness they lacked inside their religion. I always saw myself as a nice person, even when I was doing horrible things, and I feel it is this essential sense of my own goodness that drew me to darkness. Paradoxically, it is also why I could never commit to being a Christian.

Back when I decided to become a Christian, I hid my inverted cross in a jewellery box and changed the way I dressed. This was not easy, because I felt I wasn't being true to myself. One of my Christian friends said I would have to put such things away to come into a relationship with God. This put me off, because I wanted to give up these things when I was ready, not force myself into change.

It was after I decided not to become a Christian that I hallucinated a demon on top of my bookshelf, which was very strange and felt almost timely.

Letter to the Voices: Part Four
Storthes Hall
Oct 2006

Useless Apology

Balls of paper litter the floor,
Scary Mary can't write an apology,
not without your painful insinuations.
I do not intend suicide; I don't intend to pretend I have that intention.
And this is not a love letter.

Why do you talk this way?
I do not love at this time,
and the pen gliding across the page is not masturbation,
a rumour you started, to tear me away from Satan.
STOP! I'm not writing with the idea that my blood-spattered note
will be found later.

Pouring thoughts all over the place,
your rumours make me feel disgraced.
A constant tirade I cannot face,
I cannot keep up, can't win this race.
Your lies chase me,
and nothing I say or do will make it better,
I write an apology that is no love letter.

Throughout this illness you were constant and childish. The things you came up with to torment me should have been laughable and easily ignored. But though I address these letters to you as voices, there was more to my illness than just you.

There were the visual tricks you pulled, and the delusions. It was this delusional state that made what you were doing seem so real, so hurtful. In my confusion I found it difficult to address the plot holes in what you were saying about me.

A real person once asked me "How come you didn't know you were hearing voices? How come you didn't notice something was odd and go seek a doctor?" It was because of my delusional state that I didn't know you weren't real. I didn't know that what I perceived as reality was also a fabrication. The question I was asked was akin to asking a blind man why he can't see. When your mind goes fundamentally wrong, how are you supposed to be objective?

The delusion you created in me made me see no way out. Because I couldn't see the answers, I felt I was entirely to blame for my actions at the time. Even now I don't know how much was me acting, and how much was the madness you created within me. Certainly, the turmoil I felt caused some of my actions. I was dealing with emotions that were exaggerated, punctuated by times when I had no emotions at all.

It is so difficult to explain to others why someone might behave in a way that doesn't make sense. I often hear people say, "Mental health problems are no excuse for bad behaviours." But you and I know I wasn't living in the same reality as other people. I spent so much time living inside my head that eventually the inside of my head became the outside, a waking nightmare you created for me. You got me depressed and angry, annoyed and disgusted, then you dropped me a lifeline. Not a lifeline that a sane and ordinary person would cling to, but to me it felt like a reprieve from your taunts.

The lifeline came in the form of Adam. Adam was just one of your voices, but not one of the usual five. He represented a friend of yours, who I— of course—believed was another real person. Adam was convinced I was the Antichrist and was terribly afraid of me. The nastier of your voices tried to convince him that I was not to be feared, that I was deceiving him, that I was just an idiot and a wanker. He did not believe you, which meant he believed in me. This was such a strange thing to get excited about, I know.

When I was ill, I felt that if I didn't play my role correctly I would be disappointing my audience, or at least those who believed in me. I had the impression that Adam might not be sincere in his convictions about me. But I didn't care as long as he played my game.

Adam temporarily made me feel better, because he offered me a chance to escape humanness and to enter my fantasy world once again. I felt that hopefully, if I played my cards right, with his support I could get you to stop picking on me.

I'd been hearing his voice for a while, and it appeared to be coming from the flat below mine. I'd often hear you visiting his room and talking. I came to believe that Adam had been spying on me the previous year. I now had two reasons to confront him: to check if he'd spied on me and find out what he'd seen, and to get him to stop you bullying me.

While at Storthes Hall I made friends with the security staff. It was clear that they found me entertaining and amusing. I'd often be found lounging around, leaning on their desk and talking to them. On one occasion when I was chatting with them, they were called away to a fire alarm, as it was one of their jobs to check nothing was on fire. Fire alarms were a frequent occurrence at Storthes as students often burned their cooking, or on occasion intentionally set them off.

On this evening, while the security staff went to check the alarm, they left the security station unlocked. Usually they closed the shutters, so this was odd. Perhaps they assumed no one would mess with Scary Mary. As I waited for them to come back, I realised they'd left a computer on. I noticed that the display showed lists of the flats and who lived in them. So I sat in the swivel chair and took a look. I was hoping to locate where Adam lived. I searched down the list to the flat that I lived in, and then looked to the floor below. As luck would have it there actually was an Adam living on the floor below mine, in a flat to the left of my window when viewed from the outside. The presence of a real Adam made me more assured of my reality. I was convinced you were real anyway, but now I had something concrete to go on, someone I could reach. I decided to go and speak with him.

The buildings at Storthes Hall have multiple locks: a lock on the outer door, a locked inner door leading to each block of rooms, and the locked room door itself. I could open the outer lock because I lived in the same building as Adam, but for the inner door I had to knock for attention. I was afraid no one would answer the door. For a minute or so I stood waiting, then a girl answered. I stiffly asked, "Can I speak with Adam, please?"

She led me to his room. I recall that he was on his bed playing guitar with his door open. I said, "I need to speak to you privately. Could you come to my room?"

He looked confused but agreed to come. I don't know what he thought was going to happen. Perhaps he thought I was going to try and murder him, because the moment he entered my dark, red lit room, he asked "Can I turn on the main light?"

I allowed him to go ahead but pointed out that it might not make much difference. I'd covered the main light in red plastic, which made the light a sickly pink colour.

I tried to question him in a very circuitous way. I vaguely told him that the previous year someone had seen something happening in my flat. I didn't tell him what, and I certainly didn't mention Satan. Then, beating about the bush no longer, I asked, "Were you spying on me last year?"

"No," he replied. "I didn't live at that end of Storthes Hall last year."

I didn't believe him but let him go. As he turned to leave I said, "Bye Adam…", then dropped in his last name to scare him.

He looked shocked, "How did you know my last name?"

I gave him a wry smile and said nothing. After he left I hissed to myself, "He's a liar!"

True to your usual form, you used this confrontation as another way of vilifying me.

"She fancies Adam!" you'd say gleefully.

In my rapidly unravelling mind, I had as much logic as a child. I was deeply offended, and instead of brushing off what you'd said, I kept muttering that you were wrong.

At a much later date, I apologised to Adam for scaring him. Without being too specific about the circumstances leading up to it, I confessed that I'd found his name on the computer. "I shouldn't have done that." I said flatly.

I doubt he really understood what had happened.

Before this meeting, I tried to pen him an apology against a chorus of your cries.

"She's writing a love letter to Adam."

"No, she's writing a suicide note."

"She's probably just doing it for attention."

In the end I balled up the various notes I'd written and decided to speak to him in person. Which of course made things worse instead of better.

Night and day, I could hear you talking, discussing distorted versions of things that you could see in my flat, your cruelty to me being based on your mistakes. Still I was too proud to put the main light back on, even if it would mean you could see what was going on better. To do this meant to me that you had won.

Once, when it was daylight, I realised why you seemed to think I was in bed all the time. I came to realise that you must be mistaking my black clothes as me being wrapped in my black bed covers. So I decided the best way to convince you otherwise would be to make a contrast between my clothes and the bed covers. I decided to put my collection of rabbit pelts on top of the covers. Surely now you would see I wasn't in the bed wanking!

I don't know if you have independent awareness, or if you were just my mind turned feral, but do you realise how much your insinuations affected me? I can only conceive that you did, otherwise why would you have done this? The near constant barrage of hate and laughter, and the pain you caused me, drove me do such stupid things to find some solitude, solitude in your fear of me. I searched for the key to make you stop laughing and take me seriously.

Not knowing who you are is infuriating. What part of me could have become my own enemy? I have always loved myself and have no idea why you don't love me too. Could it be that you are repressed self-hatred, hate stored up from every insult people have thrown at me, the things I never felt about myself at the time, stashed away for some later date, and culminating in your torture?

After I had put my rabbit furs on the bed, I sat on my bed hoping this would be the end of the matter. Then once again I saw a dreaded flash of light from a camera. I angrily climbed on my desk to get a view out of the window to see who was spying on me. But instead of your usual laughter, this time there was a hush of terror.

From me listening to you whisper, I gathered that you'd mistaken the rabbit furs on my bed for a demon. Again, I had trouble understanding how you had seen this, since the furs were laid out flat. But it seemed likely this was another mistake made by the distance from which you were taking the photograph.

At last you were taking me seriously! I liked your fear, and I enjoyed that you'd mistaken some rabbit pelts I'd picked up cheap at a car boot sale for a demon. I was especially delighted that you had photographic evidence of my evil, evidence you were likely to share with others.

For three days I heard the rumour about the demon circulating. Or rather I heard your voices talking about me with respect and fear. There were a few who didn't believe the photograph was real, but they were in the minority. Somc of the believers planned to blackmail me with the photograph, which I found amusing.

Of course, like all things that happened between me and you, my happy state didn't last for long. What goes up must eventually come down.

One day, on the bus coming back to Storthes from uni, I saw a girl from my course, and for a change sat beside her. As we were both looking out of the window, we saw a dismembered sheep and wondered what had attacked it. I spoke to my course-mate and mentioned wanting to collect its bones to go with my collection.

As I spoke to my course-mate on the bus, I heard a nasty snigger, but thought nothing of it. When I got back to my flat, the nastiest of you—who had argued against the demon rumour throughout — said gleefully "It's a fucking dead sheep!".

My heart sank and I felt terrified, realising that no matter how improbable a dead sheep being in my flat might be, that it was more believable than a demon. I knew this new rumour would spread, and that people would see the photo in a new light. I'd go back to being tortured again.

"Devious bitch."

"Fucking deceiver!"

I pleaded with you. "Look, how would I get a dead sheep into my flat without you noticing?"

I was always trying to get through to you, but you were never swayed by my logic. To be fair, I'm not surprised. I'd tried to deceive you on so many occasions.

You kept insisting that I'd somehow brought a dead sheep into my room and, worse still, your bullying turned to mockery.

"Sheep shagger."

Even the nicer of you temporarily turned away from me, saying that I had disappointed you.

It does seem strange that I would be upset by this, because the act you accused me of was incredibly dark, but it was the way you framed it that made it upsetting. Instead of concluding that the act made me evil, you were using it as comedy, and as proof that I was a liar and an attention seeker.

At this point you'd taken to making sheep noises at me and yelling "Wanker!" at my window, laughing cruelly. I could hear you everywhere I went, and I felt deflated as your voices laughed at me and sneered.

sanity is not statistical

A Letter to Kris
Storthes Hall
Sept 2006- Feb 2008

Spider

I could not love at this time and having a partner would have cramped my style.
You did kind things for me and I barely noticed, too busy weaving my webs, making snares for everyone else except you.
You should be proud, the only one who saw through, to the person that you knew.
The only one who didn't run, from the spider I thought I was.

Where do I begin? You were the one person who recognised my rapidly worsening condition, although you didn't fully understand what was happening to me.

You first started talking to me during my second year at uni. You were a first year, and I must confess that I wasn't very impressed. I wasn't looking to make a friend and believed I could cope on my own. I thought that having friends would cramp my lone wolf style. Despite this you persisted, making every effort to be my friend, even though I was determined to be insular and behaved in a frankly narcissistic manner.

Our first meeting was at the Storthes Hall bus stop. You approached me and started talking to me. Perhaps it was my aloofness that made you feel inclined to approach. At first, I was entirely uninterested, but you kept turning up to talk to me, even though I often wasn't in the mood to talk and had nothing to say. Over time, though, you got under my armour, and I did begin to enjoy your company. We ended up spending a fair amount of time together, and we had some memorable adventures.

One excursion I remember was when you downloaded the horror film Eraserhead to your laptop. You suggested we go into the woods surrounding Storthes Hall and watch the film there in the dead of night. The woods around the immediate vicinity of Storthes were made up of small trees closely pressed together. There was a lot of foliage on the ground, which increased the spookiness of our surroundings. We ended up picking a spot on the flat roof of one of the old asylum buildings, a place that was a relic of the Hall's past. We sat on a blanket that you had provided. The night was freezing. My shivering was due to the cold, but also because I was feeling paranoid. I kept thinking we were being watched, and I was scared that someone might find us and sneak up on us. I felt the laptop light made us very visible to anyone who might want to find us. This feeling of vulnerability was heightened by the fact I was very ill, and wasn't helped by the film being the strangest I'd ever seen.

We also used to enjoy taking gothic-styled photographs of each other in various metal band poses, as if we were in a band together. We also shared a lot of music, listening to it in each other's flats. I remember you used to call my Gregorian chants and Verdi's Requiem pretentious.

It was a word you used often, but I think you were nervous and trying to impress me. You'd often bring new music you thought I'd be interested in. I also started insisting on listening to music backwards, and you very kindly would copy my music for me and reverse it. I would listen to everything back-masked regardless of whether it had lyrics. The appeal of back-masking wasn't so much for the alleged Satanic messages a person could find in the music, but in hiding what my music was. While ill I had a fascination with playing music I thought the other students wouldn't recognise, as a way to enhance my unearthly qualities. Once again, my illness had made me oblivious that you liked me in a romantic way.

You were very kind to me, despite some of the mad things I insisted we do. I have never forgotten the time when we were running round the woods making demonic screeching noises to scare the students, until you, perhaps feeling embarrassed, pointed out that the noises would be more out of place coming from my room. I agreed and we ended up listening to noise music in my flat. You also confided in me that originally when you had first seen me about campus, you hadn't really liked me, and ended up being surprised to have become my friend. You talked of fate having a hand in our meeting.

Another adventure we had together, one that I recall in detail, was when we decided to shoot some gothic photographs in the woods, in the dead of night. We took some photographs near a building that was collapsed, with no roof left. It was mostly crumbled stone walls, the moon shone down upon us.

I was wearing a long gothic coat as usual and long horns designed to look like they were sprouting from my forehead. You were in black jeans and a black hooded top and, if I recall correctly, a witch's hat.

When we had finished taking pictures, we decided to return home. We were walking along a trail covered in low creeping plants and brambles, when suddenly you crouched down behind me. I turned and laughed, "What are you doing?"

"Shh," you replied, "We're being followed."

It took me a second to process what you had said, then my heart froze, and a wave of terror ran through me. The darkness now seemed awfully dense.

When I'd collected my wits, I crouched down too, and keeping low to the ground, we both slowly made our way back to the main muddy path. My heart was hammering. I'd not seen the person who was following us, so wondered whether they were behind us or off to the side. Our progress through the brambles felt too slow for the magnitude of the situation. I was relieved when we got out of the thorny plants. The moon was obscured by the overhanging foliage, and it was darker under the trees on the path.

We both stopped and stood up. I hoped my coat hadn't snagged too much. Then we made the mistake of looking back down the path, deeper into the woods, where a figure had stepped out. He was shrouded in shadow, and we couldn't see much of him except to identify him as male. The one thing we could see clearly was that this figure was holding up an old mobile phone with the light of the screen pointed towards us. Then he started slowly advancing upon us, I could see the phone light getting closer. For few seconds—which felt like more—I stood my ground, determined not to be scared.

Then I lost my head and through gritted teeth said, "Run, Kris!" We ran away from the figure along the sludgy path. I was terrified I might trip on a tree root or slide on the mud, the whole scenario felt like something from a nightmare. I didn't dare look back to see if we were being pursued.

Eventually, panting, we made it back to the streetlamp-lit road that marked the beginning of the Storthes hall complex. We didn't say a lot on the way back to our respective flats. I felt somewhat embarrassed by the situation, worried that it had been another student messing around, who would spread the story that Scary Mary was a coward, that the bad scary goth who should have been able to defend herself ran away.

After my fear had worn off the day after, I was determined we should go back in daylight, and find evidence of student activity, because it had obviously been students mucking around, smoking dope and scaring people. I was excitable as I told you my plans to do some sleuthing, the rapid cycle of my emotions continuing to change. I was barely afraid now the moment had passed. But we didn't go back and check, because I was quite put off roaming the woods in the dark after that. This annoyed me greatly, because the darkened woods had been my domain. It was me, not others, that was supposed to do the scaring.

Being there all the way through my schizophrenic experience, watching me steadily go mad, can't have been easy for you. I was in a place where no one could reach me. That must have made you feel powerless.

I thank you for not running away, though, even when you were frustrated by my constantly changing emotions, and by my insistence that I was being bullied and watched. I still recall you trying to calm me by taking me out to the moor in your car. On the way I could hear faint voices and white noise, and everything felt hazy and unreal. You were telling me about the moors murders while we were driving along, appealing to my darker nature and trying to distract me. Under normal circumstances a person driving me to the moor and discussing the murders that happened there might have disconcerted me, but I knew you well at this point and was preoccupied by my new reality.

This conversation might have interested me more if I hadn't been convinced that the students I thought were bullying me were following us in a car. This explained why I could still hear their voices even though we were nowhere near Storthes. I can't recall if I told you that I thought we were being followed, or if I kept this thought to myself for fear that you would tell me it couldn't be true, sparking an argument.

Once, you came to my flat bringing your laptop to share some music with me. You very thoughtfully made your home screen a plain red so that it wouldn't look out of place in my red-lit room. It was a gesture I remembered because it was so sweet of you. Unfortunately, the voices decided to spoil things. They had been calling you my secret boyfriend for a while, and, as usual, were using the idea to suggest I was human. You barely had time to share your music before I made you leave my room.

I'm sorry I couldn't cope. I was so wrapped up in my own world while the voices were trying to tear it apart. They were making the world in my head a barren place where I could no longer be welcome.

I've said many times in this book that I couldn't stand the thought of being human. I think this is because I've always felt so different from others. When I was younger, I felt wiser than those around me, and had a very good grasp of what I was feeling and thinking. The people I saw around me seemed to be over-emotional and uninterested in the larger questions of the universe. They were preoccupied with making friends and fitting in, and were uninterested in everything I found important.

I lived outside of conventional norms, led by my head far more than my heart. I ran around on all fours like an animal, not caring what others had to say about it. Even though I was hurt by being excluded and bullied I never changed my ways to suit the whims of others. I have a love for myself that I don't see in many people.

Back then I was never particularly concerned about politics, and led a carefree existence, noticing only what affected me directly. These differences made me feel I wasn't human. Perhaps it was my self-separation from the human race that made it hard for me to deal with other people. It could be that they othered me in response to my othering them.

As I became more deeply psychotic, I started behaving in cruel ways towards you, trying to prove to the voices there was nothing between us. I would sometimes act as if I disliked you. I'd try and push you away, play cruel tricks, and say mean things to you. I was being tortured horribly by them, and proving them wrong seemed the only way that I could end the nightmare.

I remember going to your birthday party in 2007. It was held in the shared kitchen in your building, where some of your friends had thrown the party for you. We played kids' party games, including pin the tail on the donkey. At one point you were blindfolded and feeling your way around the room, so I picked up a bowl of jelly and held it in front of you, and you ended up dunking your hand into it. This came across as a harmless childish prank, but I was doing it to play act to the voices. I don't know what your friends made of me that night, because my behaviour was very erratic.

When I look back on my illness, much of it seems to have a dreamlike quality, as if the light was softened. It's a haze I only began to notice after I had recovered. I know the things I told you when I was ill were bizarre, and at times you couldn't grasp what I was going on about, but you never left my side.

After I had started to recover, I decided to go out with you. We ended up dating for about two months from December 2007. I had finally realised you liked me romantically, and post-illness I was feeling lonely, so I thought I'd try and have a relationship. I chose you as a partner because I thought that after sticking by me through my illness you deserved a chance.

I remember telling you that I wanted a relationship with someone, and you asked me if I had considered you. I replied that I had planned to ask you. You then leaned over and kissed me, which was when I realised I'd made a mistake. This wasn't because of anything you did, but it just occurred to me that I wasn't ready. I didn't break things off then and there, though, because I figured I should at least give the relationship some time.

My sense that I wasn't ready for a relationship at this point was soon proved correct. I was only in the very early stages of recovery, and I was in shock. To further compound my problems, the first medication I was prescribed was an antipsychotic called Olanzapine. This medication had a profoundly sedative effect upon me and made it hard to function normally. I describe being on it as feeling like a zombie. I needed to sleep a lot, not only because of the medication, but because my brain was recovering from the illness. My waking hours were blurry, and I couldn't think straight, or even attempt to pursue hobbies like I used to. I also didn't have the presence of mind to make a relationship work, which was a shame. You were a nice person and had been a good friend to me.

I was not very attentive to our relationship and was tired all the time. It was when I was visiting you at your student house in Huddersfield that I'd also go and visit the church and see my friends. This was partly because I didn't know what to do about our relationship and felt that I needed some time away from you.

I feel you may have been distressed at the change in me. From being talkative and exuberant I became withdrawn and quiet. I could barely find the words to express myself, and so we usually defaulted to watching TV shows or listening to music together. Sometimes I felt that you didn't understand the impact the illness had upon me. You tended to joke about it, a coping mechanism you turned to well before I was ready to see any humour in my situation.

Another thing that put me off our relationship was you subtly pressuring me for sex. You'd told me you would wait as long as it took me to be ready, but you'd do things to try to and get me interested in the notion, such as showing me porn of girls allegedly losing their virginity. Porn really did nothing for me, because the environments in the videos seemed too sterile, the acting was crap, and the budgets too low to portray anything I was interested in.

In 2008 I attended your next birthday party, which was a much more subdued affair, just us and two friends and some home-made absinthe. You and your friends were smoking weed, and you offered me some, but I declined. "Why not?" you asked, "You're mad anyway."

I was sorely tempted to take you up on the offer of dope, but this was because I felt betrayed by my brain. I'd looked after myself as best I knew how and ended up being tortured by the organ I most relied on. My desire was an act of self-sabotage that I fortunately didn't give in to. I knew that weed could make my symptoms worse, so contented myself with drinking home-made absinthe, which nearly made me throw up.

It was at my twenty-first birthday party that I finally decided to break it off with you. You seemed depressed on that night and this was the catalyst for our breakup. My party was very lively. It was at my house, where I lived with mum, and all my friends and family showed up. I don't know if you were jealous that night, but you hid yourself away and didn't socialise very much. I decided then that I wasn't capable of love because I wasn't feeling any normal emotions related to our relationship. I thought it would hurt you less if I ended things sooner rather than later.

Recently we've spoken again through Facebook, and I am grateful there are no hard feelings between us, and that you are happy with your wife. I am also happily married and will take you up on your offer to visit your home in Huddersfield. After all my turbulent times at university I've avoided going back there because of the memories surrounding my illness. But I shall return to meet with you, my old friend.

A Letter to Ryan
Doncaster/ Storthes Hall
2003- 2009

Attention!

Look at me, do you not see,
the colours that bleed out of me,
when you use those words.

Depleting me of why I do this,
making me seem ludicrous,
those words like a wound.

Do you not see how nervous I am,
when I try a new approach,
I don't mean to encroach on your time.

I've spent lengthy hours, hiding from eyes,
wearing a disguise,
yet surprise, surprise,

you use those words again to describe me.

Time and again I've heard them,
red raw, until my ears are sore,
a way of misunderstanding me.

All because I won't pander to you,
to societies sensibilities,
if you were inquisitive, you might ask why?

But instead of seeking answers,
to questions to tough to mention,
instead you simply say, that she's seeking attention.

We don't speak any more. After what happened with my illness our friendship fell apart. The last time I saw you was when I invited you to my twenty second birthday party. To your credit you did show up, but we barely said a word to one another.

I met you in sixth form, you dressed in an alternative style too, so we became friends, you were slightly intrigued by me I realised, despite the fact you had a girlfriend. You saw all of my exuberant behaviour in sixth form, but it didn't seem to bother you, my mad antics were never brought up.

Though we spent a lot of time hanging out, at school we mostly saw each other in the art room or the common room. You liked to paint pictures of cars, and they were quite realistic looking, but cars were never my interest. I'd paint elaborate surrealist scenes that seemed to impress you and the other students. I enjoyed talking to you during art, and we shared the various music we were into. You, I recall were a big Cradle of Filth fan, and you used to share their albums with me. It took a while for me to get into Cradle of Filth, given the screaming lyrics and rapid pace of the music, but once I was used to it, I did enjoy them.

We would go to lots of social events together, and at one party we ended up kissing. That was actually a fairly wild party, the strange thing was despite the fact you had a girlfriend I didn't feel guilty about kissing you on that occasion. It was only afterwards when a friend found out and told your girlfriend what had happened that I felt incredibly guilty. It was as if the guilt only came once I'd been caught out.

I apologised to your girlfriend for what I'd done, and I can't remember if this is when your relationship dissolved, or if I'm misremembering.

Though I wasn't romantically attached to you, I could recognise that there was something between us, though I was keen not to go out with anyone from school. I used to feel embarrassed at the thought of people finding out that I'd kissed you, and on one occasion your girlfriend, though you knew about that. I did not want people to think I was being a hypocrite or misunderstand that because I'd had vague teenage sexual encounters, that it meant I was ready to romantically connected to another.

Funnily enough we both ended up applying to the same university course at Huddersfield and ended up on the art course together. When we first arrived you were very nervous, and seemed to cling to me a bit. For you however university made you grow as a person and become more confident over time, whereas I was robbed of this opportunity by my illness.

You seemed to make friends easily and ended up with a new girlfriend, very few people stayed my friend. And even now I have very few people from uni who I regularly stay in touch with. I feel as if I came away from university having made no friends, even though there are a few people I do sometimes talk to from my days there.

As time went on you seemed to drift away, spending more time with your new friends.

Whereas I drifted into my own fantasy world.

During my second year, when I made the 'Scary Mary' thread with the aid of my friend, many people commented, including a comment by you, your comment came after the comment of the girl who accused me of being an attention seeker.

Your comment said this, "I agree, I'm her friend and even I think she an attention seeker." This comment cut through me like ice and I ended up crying, and though I didn't think a lot about this comment at the time, because I was dealing with the voices, later on I realised how hurt I'd been by it. It makes me wonder, given how I'd behaved in school, for how long had you been thinking this? Was the thought always there, but you just waved aside because you fancied me? Or was it a realisation after what I did that day?

I rarely saw much of you after that point, except on the art course. One day when the voices were particularly bad, I was in the art room singing, you were there painting, I was singing to show the voices I had talent, and to stop them mocking me, I was going for it a bit, singing high passages from Phantom of the Opera. When suddenly you turned around and aggressively roared at me to "Shut the fuck up!"

I fell silent as the voices laughed at me, and said "If she was really evil she'd have carried on."

I was hurt by your words and was in such a bad place that I had no will to argue. I felt ashamed and embarrassed that you had said that to me, and couldn't concentrate on my artwork. I sat on the floor and painted images into my book 'the rules of engagement.' and didn't wait for them to dry properly before closing the pages.

Though I tell myself that you couldn't have known I was ill, and that to you it would have appeared that I was just attention seeking, I can't bring myself to forgive you for shouting those words at me when I was in the darkest of places, and I was pained and hurt by losing a friend, one whom I never truly realised was slipping away from me.

Letter to the Voices: Part Five
Storthes Hall
Oct 2006- Nov 2006

The Lowest Point

I fell into this hole, the lowest point,
afraid I'd disappoint you, so afraid to be me.
Giving way to lunacy.
There is no way back up from this,
I know the only way is down, down, down.
I wear my smile to show you it is a fallacy,
you can't stop me, please don't stop me!
I draw, and you draw blood, I sit and pretend that all is good,
and all according to fantasy.

One evening while I was outside doing some gymnastics, I was approached by a very drunk girl. She spoke nastily to me and accused me of being on drugs. I was hurt and offended by this. I may have dressed differently, but of course this didn't automatically mean I took drugs. Indeed, at the time I saw drug use as weakness. But her remarks were the only cue you needed, because it was then that you started accusing me of being on drugs.

"She's obviously on drugs." you'd sneer.

If I coughed or sneezed, it was because I was on drugs, or that coughing was a way of getting your attention.

"Attention seeker."

"Fucking drugged up bitch!"

This was not the only game you had in store for me. The next one was centred on my cooking. I've always been proud of my cooking skills, but while I was in the shared kitchen making my dinner your taunts turned to, "Look at her, she's pretending to know what she's doing!"

This upset and annoyed me, and it was your constant questioning of my abilities and hurtful statements that caused me to stop cooking and eating properly. In the end I had a subsistence diet of bread, chocolate, fruit, milk and occasionally meat that I'd never cook properly, since I always wanted to get out of the kitchen as fast as possible.

There was a time when I was in the kitchen when the believers amongst you thought I'd stuck my hand into boiling water. In reality it was moderately warm water, and I'd put my hand into it to fish out a hair. Of course, this became a big argument between those of you that wanted to deify me, and those that wanted to vilify me. Was I evil because I managed to withstand the temperature of the water? Or was it all a massive trick?

On one occasion I ate a half-frozen steak. Some of you suggested that my eating raw meat meant I was the Antichrist, whereas others pointed out that I would make myself ill. In my distress at your constant bullying and speculation, I called Kris. Kris invited me over to watch South Park the Movie, so I happily went round to his place to get my mind off things.

I really enjoyed watching the film, having never seen it before. The only thing that distracted me from it was hearing your voices saying, "What the hell is she watching?" and questioning why I was laughing. After the film, I asked Kris quite innocently, "Can I use your bathroom?"

That was all you needed to hear, because then, howling with laughter, you suggested that I had diarrhoea because of the raw meat I'd eaten earlier in the day. This, of course, proved I was human.

As I left Kris's and walked back to my block, I could hear you all laughing and calling each other up on the phone to share the shameful news. Some of you made owl noises at me as I walked. I felt disgusted and hateful of humanity for being such idiots, and for treating something like this— especially since it was untrue—as news.

I went up to my room and sat on my bed. All around me I could hear you howling at me in mocking voices, telling me to go to the toilet.

"Have a shit, you daft bitch!"

I felt the lowest I'd ever been. I often refer to this time as, 'The Lowest Point' when I depict it in my artwork, even though later my feelings and moods sank even lower.

I tried so hard to ignore your taunts. I started painting pictures and doing drawings, sitting on the bed under the red light's glow, but this didn't work.

"Your artwork is shit!" you shouted repeatedly.

I rushed my pictures to completion, hoping that when you saw them finished, you'd see they were good, but no matter what I did you continued to torment me. After a few hours I really did start feeling the need to go to the toilet, but I held off, because I knew you would laugh at me if I went. I resisted the urge and kept drawing.

"She's fucking drawing pictures to keep us watching her."

"How can she tell what colours she's using in that light?"

"She's trying to tell us something."

"Attention seeking bitch."

"Kill yourself."

Eventually I gave in and went to the toilet but made sure I was as quick about it as possible, to prove I didn't have diarrhoea. I was absolutely disgusted at you and at the rest of humanity. On every shout of "kill yourself!" you'd laugh nastily, as if telling someone to commit suicide is funny, or just a bit of a joke. So I started playing a game with you. There was a large knife on my desk, near my chalice. The knife had been left there from a time when I'd been cutting up a mango. I ate most things in my room because I didn't like people to see me eat, again because of the humanness of the act.

The game I started was this. I would lunge towards the knife, as if I was going to kill myself, but at the last minute I'd grab my chalice and take a drink from it. It was a game which only ended up deepening my hatred of humanity, because every time I lunged towards the knife, I'd hear the gleeful cry of "She's going to do it!"

Then when it turned out I wasn't about to kill myself, you'd groan in disappointment and shout "Attention seeker!"

"Bitch."

"Wanker."

Eventually I grew so despondent I decided to close my curtains so you wouldn't be able to see in. But when I closed my curtains, I found a strange thing: you could still see me through the closed curtains. I reasoned that either you could see me through the tiny gap in the middle where the curtains didn't quite come together, or that you were spying on me with infrared cameras pointed at my flat, reading my heat signature.

I climbed up on my desk and hung a piece of black fabric from the curtain rail to close the gap. I didn't get chance to figure out what I could do about the infrared cameras because, right after I put the cloth up, a cry went up. One of you shouted, "She's wanking in front of the window." I realised that you must think the cloth was me standing at the gap in the curtains, so I immediately tore it down and opened my curtains again.

There was the inevitable debate among you. One of your voices said that I'd been floating when I was at the window; the cloth hadn't reached all the way down when I'd hung it, and that it meant I had some sort of supernatural powers. I couldn't win no matter what I tried to do. I pleaded with you to come to my flat so that I could explain myself and sort the whole thing out.

"Attention seeking bitch!" you cried, as I begged you to come and discuss the matter with me. I called up Kris's flat and told him what had been happening, that everyone was laughing and saying I had diarrhoea, but his response was a disappointed "I thought you didn't care what others thought of you."

Then to my absolute horror, you started discussing my madness. One of you suggested ringing the asylum, as it was the only way to stop me deceiving you. I heard you in your flat discussing the matter, then I heard you on the phone.

"Hi… yeah, we've got a mad girl up here… Storthes Hall. Yeah, she shagged a dead sheep, and she wanks in front of the window."

I was not aware at the time, that a bunch of 'students' calling a mental health facility on behalf of someone they don't know is not how anybody becomes sectioned. In my maddened state, I also didn't realise how this conversation had sounded. If a real person had called a mental health facility using those words, they would not have been taken seriously. But I was stripped of all rationale by my illness and couldn't think properly.

At the time I felt awful, I kept imagining being picked up and taken away in a white van with blacked-out windows, and it looked to me that this was going to happen. I imagined over and over having to call my mum to tell her I'd been locked up. I assumed the asylum would be like a prison, and I'd be limited to choosing one person to call.

I felt tragic and lay on the bed despairing. I planned what I should do the following day when the people from the asylum would be coming to pick me up. There was a small element of hope mingled in with my fear, hope that if I could convince the men in white to listen to me, then I could sort the whole thing out. They might even realise you were bullying me, and that it was all a fabrication and a mistake. After all, it wasn't as though I was mad.

te e I hate e I hate e I hate e I
te e I hate e I hate e I hate
e I hate e I hate e I hate e I hate
I hate e I [illegible] e I hate e
hate e [illegible] e I hate e
e e I hate e [illegible] e I hate e
te e I hate e I hate e I hate
te e I hate e I hate e I hate e
e I hate e I hate e I hate e I
e I hate e I hate e I
e I hate e I hate e I
e I hate e I hate e I
e I hate e I hate e I
e I hate e I hate e I hate e
e I hate e I hate e I hate e I
e I hate e I hate e I hate e I
te e I hate e I hate e I hat
e I hate e I hate e I hate e I h

A Letter to LaVey
Doncaster
The Present

The Spaces in Between

We are nothing, you and I,
a set of atoms swirling with electrons.
Spaces so vast, that we are emptiness,
humanity with no spaces would fit into a matchbox,
with room left to spare.

Space is empty, emptier than we can gather,
planets swirling round like electrons,
in a vast empty void,
once crushed into a single point, the eye of a god.

We are something, you and I,
a set of atoms swirling with electrons.
We have mass, not see through like glass,
humanity without spaces, would be closer than we've ever been.

Space is full, fuller than we realise,
planets swirling round like electrons.
A place full of light,
almost like a brain, the brain of a god.

You died in 1997 when I was ten. Your death was quite some time before I even knew you existed, so I never had the chance to tell you how much I did respect the psychology and cleverness of your writings, even if I now don't agree with most that is in them.

Until recently I would have justified myself through LaVeyan

Satanism purely because when explaining Satanism I usually started by explaining your outlook, partly because explaining your take was a good way of explaining that Satanism does not include blood sacrifice. I do not need to do this any more since I'm no longer a Satanist. Don't get me wrong, I really enjoyed your books and teachings, but a lot of soul searching has taught me that I believe in the unseen far more than you did. My sceptical questioning side loved what you had to say, and it was precisely this side of me which caused me so much religious confusion. As I have said, I wanted to believe in your teachings and in Christian theology. But my agnostic streak won't permit me to embrace faith completely. I feel strongly that everything should be questioned, and that we should be slow to believe, whatever agenda people are pushing.

In the past I viewed those who believed without questioning as fools, and I am still very careful about repeating views as if they are certain and concrete. I realise now, though, that I was imperfectly aligned with you. I do believe in something more than you did. I have few specific convictions, but I believe that there is something else beyond this material reality, and something more to search for.

However I feared that I wouldn't be taken seriously by your followers if I should say "actually, I do feel there is more to life than just death and random cosmic accidents."

This is not a rejection or invalidation of your viewpoints, I still find somethings that are valid in the framework of your religion. I still enjoy revisiting your books and find your critiques of mainstream religion very interesting. Though I have come to realise there is more politics in your books than on the surface. When I used to read them I only saw one direct mention of politics, so took your books as separate from politics, however I see now, a lot of your world view relates to politics, and not particularly politics I agree with.

Your church was set up around the time that the Black Panther movement was growing, and I wonder if this could be why you suggest in your doctrine that a person should not sacrifice themselves to a cause. There was a lot going on politically around that time that I had previously been unaware of.

I hold one belief that is quite similar to Christian thinking. I believe that when we reach the next plane of existence, we learn all there is to know about the previous plane. This is like the Christian teaching of being judged by God after death. This is why I want my account of events to be truthful. Every time one of my relatives or friends dies, I believe they know my story in full, and perhaps even know it better than I do, due to the limitations of my earthly memory.

I don't like to lie, even though I am aware that in some situations tact is required. It seems ridiculous when in the end the people I know will find out every truth about me, and I everything about them. With this knowledge comes understanding, of course. How can a person judge someone when they themselves are facing judgement?

This sounds at odds with the way I behaved, given that I likened myself to a deceiver. But deception was my way around my truthfulness. While I feel uncomfortable making up lies, it didn't seem to matter if I could make people create the lies themselves.

When I was an agnostic Satanist, I wondered why I would take such a risk with my soul. The stakes were high, because if I was wrong about the way things played out, then my soul would have gone to hell. My answer to myself was all religions come with a similar risk. Practically every religion says there are consequences for getting things wrong. All things being equal, I figured I might as well choose what I wanted to do. After all I reasoned Satan might not be the bad guy. Propaganda is found everywhere.

I have always felt there is a massive hypocrisy in me when I deal with thoughts of the supernatural. I seem to believe in the supernatural more profoundly when I apply it to myself. If someone else tells me they are psychic or an empath, I tend to be polite, but aware of all the flaws and contradictions in what the person has told me. Whereas when I apply such thoughts to myself, I accept more easily that there could be truth in the possibility of supernatural powers. I have also wondered if being mentally ill confers supernatural abilities. I know these ideas would be spiritual pipe dreams to you, but I can't help believing in the supernatural as at least a possibility. After all, I have been through so many strange experiences.

Some of your articles were well ahead of their time, but as I've grown as a person, I find I don't agree with as much of what you said. Your writings are insightful, but still I find myself disagreeing with more of your work over time. Though now I have shed the notion of myself as a Satanist, despite holding onto some beliefs I feel freer.

A letter to the Bullies in Sixth Form
Doncaster
Sept 2003 – April 2005

I Can't Stop Being Entertaining

A wind-up monkey with cymbals clash,
why do I always act so rash?
I love myself and who I am,
but my designs did not always go as planned.

I knew of your hatred through and through, but was it really hatred though?

Those who claim to hate Satanism,
Don't see they're really trapped in a prison.
One of their own lies and making,
your hatred often seemed like faking.

You like this world as much as me, but you couldn't admit to this and here's the twist.

The reason I was entertaining to you,
is because you love my world, you know it's true.
From the other side you come,
your hatred knows no bounds and then some.

But you revel in secrets, join in with my games, and that is why I entertain.

You treated me as if I were a monkey, someone who existed solely for your entertainment. Admittedly I didn't do myself many favours. I was so excited about Satanism that I felt a compulsion to discuss it with all and sundry.

There is a chapter in The Devil's Notebook by LaVey called, 'Let Me Entertain You', which sets out how to avoid being seen as entertaining. The two methods outlined entail either boring your audience with long-winded details or disappointing your quarry by appearing comical and frivolous. It's good advice, but it's advice I did not follow and had no intention of following. At the time I was something of a showman, I was more akin to Crowley than LaVey.

I often behaved exuberantly, like I was unaware that you were trying to bully me. You conducted your bullying in a covert fashion, with a smile on the face and an arm around the shoulders, feigning interest and friendship. I was aware you were trying to bully me, and trying to make me look stupid, but in my steadily deepening madness I didn't really care. All I desired was to play games with you, to come across in such an odd manner that you would believe in the world I was creating.

There were things I did without rhyme or reason, such as entering the common room one day and spontaneously doing gymnastics moves or spitting fake blood at you. In my world I sought the company of others I believed wanted to play the game with me. These were people that validated the notions I had of myself. So when people dodged out of my way, when they saw me coming down the school corridor, I took this as them wanting to believe in my world and would specifically target my efforts towards them.

Because some of you behaved in this way, I felt as though you were interested and wanted to join me in my world. I couldn't care less that you were attempting to bully me. So long as you played your roles correctly, acted afraid of me when I did odd things, and were intrigued by me, then we could get on.

Often you would ask me about Satanism, but despite my burning desire to discuss it I would start to act coy and would tell you nothing of value. This served to obscure the shakiness of my ideas around this time, and at the same time enabled me to feel mysterious by withholding information.

I knew that some of you thought of me as an attention seeker, responding perhaps to the erratic way I behaved. This was a source of internal conflict to me, because at the time I wondered if it could be true. I'd been battered with this term so many times, and my behaviour seemed to point this way, after all how could I cause fear if you were unaware of me? Attention seeker was a term I hated, partly because of my own internal concerns. Would I even be a goth if no one cared? I consoled myself with the notion that people would notice me anyway regardless of how I dressed, "I am not invisible," I'd tell myself, but the conflict was still there within me. I have come to realise that seeking attention is not always a bad thing. How is someone supposed to get help if they don't ask someone to attend to them?

In our social media-driven world people are often looking for attention, likes, or praise, but we would not turn round and label these people attention seekers. No: attention seeker is a label unjustly reserved for that which scares us and that which we don't understand.

Social media makes me uncomfortable. I still share my artwork through it, but I cringe and feel nervous when I start attracting attention on social media platforms. This has made me realise that the label people have in the past attached to me for being different is not an accurate one. Ironically, a lot of people who have labelled me an attention seeker are often to be found on social media doing just that.

You may be mortified that I have labelled you as bullies, because you probably felt you were just having a laugh or experimenting to see what I might do, or impressing your mates by goading me. I am aware that my exuberance and over-the-top manner is what caused you all to bully me. But my being different was no good reason to steal from me, or throw water over me, or hurl rocks and food at me after school. You didn't know I was going insane at the time, but neither did I.

The only reason I behaved this way was because of this illness. The too-intense emotions I felt towards the things I was into caused me to want to share them. Had I been sane around this time, I might have been able to keep myself to myself and concentrate on lessons. It's even possible I may not have become a Satanist in the first place.

Religiosity— where a person becomes deeply interested in religion—is a symptom that some people with schizophrenia develop. For many the religion they choose is one of the more mainstream faiths. For me it happened to be Satanism, and I'm not totally sure why.

As a child I always liked baddies, and predatory animals. A part of me somewhere within wanted to be a predator. I have a sense that being frightening was the only way I could reclaim back some power, power which all the bullies in my life had taken away.

I first noticed my delight at causing fear when I was young. A girl at primary school asked me whether it was true that I had rabies. I assume she thought this because I was running on all fours, so instead of allaying her fears, I started snarling at her, chasing her and lunging at her.

Often people at school would ask me questions such as, "do you like Hitler?". I didn't say a lot at the time knowing that if I said no, then you'd question the validity of my religion. Back when I was in sixth form, I never had any political leanings, though I did hold what I realise now would have been considered some extreme right-wing views, more driven by what the media told me rather than by any understanding.

I used to think of war as good entertainment, having never had to live through one. I didn't realise what a privileged viewpoint this was at the time. These days politically I still don't regard myself as either left or right leaning, this because I feel these terms are defunct.

Where Hitler was concerned, I never thought of him as cool or interesting, partly because he was human, and prone to the weaknesses of the human condition. I always saw human evil as driven by weaknesses such as lust, hunger for power, anger, fear or envy. I seemed to view the evil of Lucifer as purer and more considered than human evil, not driven by weaknesses. Perhaps I was aligning Lucifer's character with my own, almost as if I felt he was thinking with his head instead of his heart. I no longer try to appear evil, since this behaviour was largely a product of my illness.

I always feel that the people who hated me for my religion were the people who loved it the most. These people bullied me but were also afraid of me, and I think they liked it that way. They liked the idea of my darkened world, a world that is often associated with secrets and covert operations.

Recently I read an article in a newspaper that claimed a dog walker had stumbled on a group of people performing a Satanic ritual in the woods. The newspaper was quick to report that when visiting the scene, they had found no evidence of such goings-on. But they still printed the article anyway, because the lack of evidence adds to the mystique of the story. I feel that people I was in school with shared this approach. I was an easy target, one you claimed to hate. This was partly because you would also be bullied if you didn't hate me too, but I was an excellent source of entertainment, gossip and speculation.

People like to believe in other worlds. I don't doubt my fantastical behaviour made a fair few of you excited about the prospect of a shadowy world, one you weren't a part of, but that gave you a sense of excitement, mystique and wonder.

Most of my odd behaviour in sixth form was aimed at maintaining and living within my fantasy realm, a world where I was definitely not human, where I was a supernatural force to be reckoned with. I knew more about your treatment of me than I let on, but to acknowledge it wasn't part of my narrative.

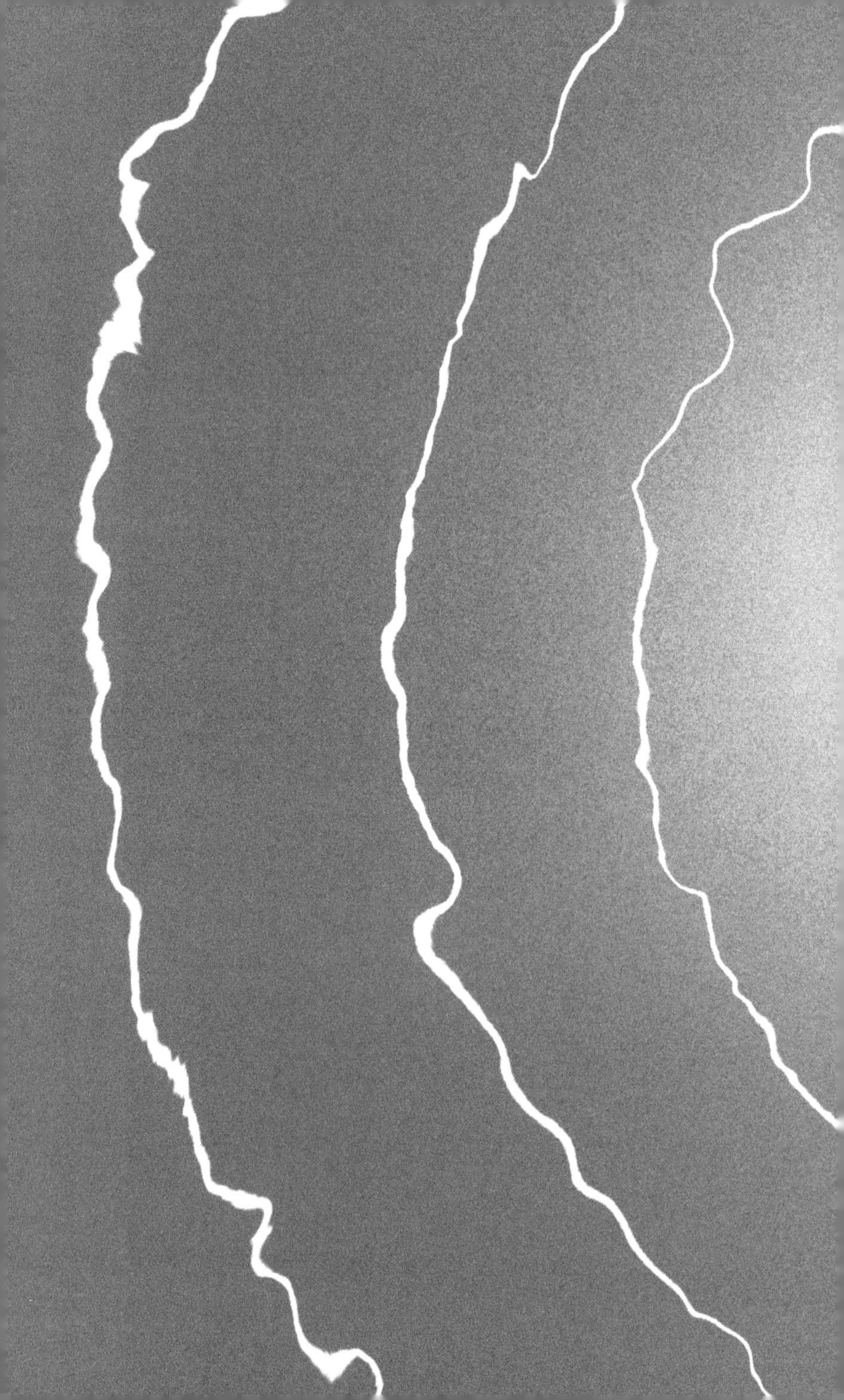

Part Two

Hell Here

Letter to the Voices: Part Six
Storthes Hall
Nov- 2006

The Fourth Storey Window

I wish the night was quiet, but there you are again.
Mocking me, as I stand here, contemplating my fall.
From grace? Or in the imagination, as I plunge into the void?
If I were to fall would that be enough?
To end this torment, or would I create more?

I'm here because of you.
Incessantly, constantly you.
An assassination of my character.
Your words haunt me, in the dark, in the day.

If I were to fall would that be enough?
Would I end this torment?
Your voice shouting "Attention seeker."
Makes me turn away.

The day after I heard you'd called the asylum, I decided to dress down while still maintaining a look that was true to my image. I powered my face white as usual and lined my eyes. I picked what I thought was my most non-offensive gothic coat and wore it over black jeans and a black shirt, with a pair of black shoes. I kept my inverted cross on but didn't wear horns or my articulated claw rings. I felt like I was dressing for my funeral.

I chose to wear my shoes in case I had to fight, run, or even comply with the people who might come to take me. I guessed I'd be the compliant sort when the people finally came, and this thought made me want to cry. There were many times during my illness that I wanted to cry but couldn't, probably because of the terrible stress I was under.

So I sat on my bed and waited for a white van to pull up, one with blacked-out windows, like one I'd seen before in the town centre. At least, I thought, if they came for me I could explain to them that I was perfectly normal and try make it clear that this was all a huge mistake. Perhaps, I reckoned, when the people realised I was being bullied, they would get you to come and talk to me, and they could clear this mess up.

I waited and waited, with no thought of going into uni for lectures, wondering when they would show up. I could hear you commenting on me. While I was waiting, I sat stiffly on my bed, with my hands in my lap. With my eyes focused straight ahead unblinking, I barely moved, trying not to provoke further reaction from you. I tried hard not to show my dread. I kept getting up to look out of the window, thinking I'd heard a van pulling up.

Eventually the dreaded crows started cawing and circling the sky, looking for roosting spots. As night closed in, and I put my red light back on, I realised that you had tricked me. You hadn't called the asylum - you had just pretended to. My hopes at sorting out the situation were dashed, and I felt despair.

To try and communicate with you I started writing signs, putting them where you could see them. They were scribbled in biro or painted in black acrylic paint, in big, bold capital letters. They said things like:

"Just come and talk to me!"

"Stop spying on me! This is not a zoo."

"Stop assuming things."

On the sign which said stop assuming things, you insisted that I had spelt assuming wrong and I believed I had, so I re-wrote 'assuming' with one s instead of two. You laughed raucously, mocking that I couldn't spell.

The signs didn't work. All they had managed to do was elicit cries of "Attention seeker" from you, or "You'll just deceive us if we talk to you."

"Freak."

"Wanker."

I lay down on the bed to rest. Then you started saying that the rise and fall of my chest meant I was masturbating, so I tried to breathe as shallowly as possible to stop you accusing me. In the end, giving up hope, I shut the curtains, hoping you would stop. Suddenly, from the room above, I heard a loud bang. It was a brief sound just like something heavy being dropped. Then I heard your mocking laughter, followed by "Oh my God, she's killed herself."

"Stupid bitch."

"Serves her right for deceiving us!"

"Told you she's human."

Livid and trembling, I felt a deep sick rage and absolute disgust that people would laugh over a potential suicide. The knowledge was deep within me that if it had been anyone else who'd killed themselves then you wouldn't be laughing. Your vile mirth was purely because it was me. Your laughter was always so cruel.

Then a dilemma presented itself to me. I had the idea that I could pretend I was dead, at least for one night, just so I could get some peace, and maybe even sleep. But the problem I faced was that next day I was supposed to go to a lecture. I could either tell you I wasn't dead and face your wrath now, or I could get some respite but face worse torment in the morning when you realised I was alive and well.

After some deliberation I decided to come clean. I thought that if I told the truth you might stop calling me a deceiver, so I began to call up random numbers on the internal landline. At Storthes, each flat had an internal phone number consisting of four digits, so it wasn't too much effort for me to try and ring a few. To me it didn't matter whose flat numbers they were, because I knew you would find out I was alive no matter who I told, since everyone was talking about me.

The first few numbers I called went unanswered, which served only to increase my sense of frustration. Finally, someone picked up. I didn't explain myself, but simply said in a hurried voice, "Hi, it's Scary Mary. I'm not dead." Then I hung up.

I have no idea what the person on the receiving end of this strange call thought. The main thing was that as soon as I put the phone down you got the message. Your reaction was not the one I wanted, however. I had thought you might be a bit more forgiving, bearing in mind I'd told the truth. I couldn't win, though, because you started spreading the rumour that I'd faked my own suicide for attention. I had terrible feelings of guilt.

Guilt was a constant companion during my schizophrenic experience. I always felt that everything I did was my bad judgement, and not a reasonable reaction to what you were saying about me. It was as if I couldn't do right in your eyes. Even telling you the truth was wrong.

"Did you hear? She pretended to commit suicide for attention."

"Fucking deceiver."

"Devious bitch!"

There was a distinct pattern to the way things played out

between me and you. Each cycle would start with you seeing something in my room. I'd try and convince you it wasn't true—especially if I thought it was a bad thing you'd seen—but you'd ignore my pleas. If, however, I thought it was a good thing you'd seen, then I'd keep silent, knowing through your fear you'd treat me with respect. Then disaster would strike, you'd realise what you had seen was a mistake on your part, and you'd blame me for not having told the truth.

It never occurred to me that a gang of students wouldn't necessarily make me the centre of their world or be spying on me. This thinking was in part due to how I saw myself, the importance I attributed to my existence. Of course people were going to spy on me and talk about me, because I was so different to everybody else.

To prove I didn't care about anything, I would chew up tissue paper and spit it at the wardrobe in my room. On one occasion, to frighten you, I surreptitiously took a mouthful of fake blood and spat it at my window. It hit the glass in a big splat. A small blob landed on my picture of Lucifer, which caused you to laugh at me. I was of course very upset that this had happened.

I would sit in my flat and write the words 'I hate' and 'I hate' and 'I hate' over and over because you made me feel hateful of humanity. I believed the whole of humanity hated me too, and that they were stupid and gullible fools. I believed everyone was invested in my torture, that you were spying on me and laughing at me, urging everyone else to sneer at me.

Hatred was a common emotion while I was ill. My feelings were amped up, and much stronger than regular emotions at the time. My hatred felt like a mixture of anger and disgust, and it was powerful. Instead of being merely angry I was livid and raging. If I became upset, I'd feel despair, a dark pit with no feeling of hope at the end. And if I became happy, I was ecstatic and trembling with glee. The emotional changes I went through were the hardest part of the illness to cope with. The emotions you made me feel were agonising, and they were sometimes so bad that they manifested themselves as nausea or physical pain.

The day after I gave you my proof that I was alive, I went out to study at university as planned, amidst your shouts of "Attention seeker." Even on the bus I could hear you referring to me as a sheep shagger, and I could feel tears forming. I turned my face away from the crowds on the bus so that nobody would see me cry. This was tricky because on the bus rides to and from university I'd avoid looking out of the windows so as not to appear to be looking at the sheep in the fields.

When I arrived at the art room, I could still hear you, and became convinced you were spying on me through the skylight from a taller building on the university site. There was just one problem to add to my confusion: every time I looked up at the ceiling there was no skylight. But when I looked back down at my work, I was convinced it was there, and that you were spying on me through it. I could hear you commenting on my artwork, so it must be there. I couldn't put this feeling out of my head. Every time I looked up at the ceiling I'd feel confused, but not confused enough to question my perception. Seeing there was no skylight didn't even spark fear or alarm within me. This was flat affect, the deadening of my emotions because of schizophrenia. Where emotions were concerned it was all or nothing.

My reality was distorted to such a degree while I was ill that I knew the skylight was there but had no explanation when it turned out I was wrong. I was certain you must be spying on me because I could hear you. I never even mentioned the 'skylight' to the people who were in the art room with me.

After I'd finished in the art room and I went to get the bus back to Storthes Hall, I felt strangely confounded because there was no tall building near the art room. But, as with the skylight, I just shelved my deepening confusion, and couldn't grasp the obvious evidence that no one could possibly be spying on me.

When I got home to my flat, I pleaded with you to come and talk to me so we could sort out the whole mess. After much shouting and cruelty from you, I closed my curtains again. To my enormous upset, another loud bang issued from the flat above me, and I was forced to open my curtains to prove I was alive and not trying to kill myself. Of course, this didn't work, because you just accused me of trying the same trick again.

"She's done it again."

"The stupid bitch."

Had I been able to apply any sort of logic I would have realised you couldn't possibly have thought this. After all, I'd opened my curtains almost immediately after hearing the bang. I tried to get you to talk to me again, but you refused, so I resolved to take matters into my own hands. I planned to run up to the fourth storey of the building, because I sometimes heard your voices up there.

I banged on the internal door of the fourth floor in a vain attempt to get someone to heed me. All the while I could hear your voices laughing and saying, "We're not going to talk to you". I felt a sense of utter despair wash over me. I couldn't even cry because I was so tired and distressed. I went over to the window in the corridor, the one that looked out over Storthes Hall, and pushed it open. Something must have been broken in the window frame, because there was nothing to stop me opening the window wide. I looked out into the night sky, feeling the cold air and a slight breeze playing on my face. The night was cloudless. I considered throwing myself out of the window, and for once my head felt alarmingly quiet.

I paused, trying to weigh up the possibilities. If I fell from a height of four storeys, would I merely injure myself, or would I die? Perhaps I'd end up brain damaged. The very real prospect of not finishing the job 'properly' made me stop. Then one of you piped up "She's going to jump for attention."

This shouted statement made me reconsider my options. I didn't want my legacy to be shaped by you. I had a compulsion to prove to you that you were wrong about me. Reluctantly I trudged back down the stairs, back to my flat, to endure another night of pain and torture.

A Letter to Rosie
Doncaster
1991-Present

The Fairy Delusion

I saw her hanging there.
In front of my face, dangled in air.
Like a ballet dancer, tiny and perfect.
Arms raised above her head.
Wings out, splayed.
One leg making movements.
As if about to dance.
I stared entranced.
Unbelieving at the little being.
I didn't believe what I was seeing.
I stared hard, and the penny dropped.
The delusion broke.
I recoiled in shock.
My eyes locked with the arachnid.
I realised my mistake.
The deception my eyes had played.
Delusion is where dreams are made.

I feel as though you haven't quite forgiven me for the way I treated you before I was ill. I got on better with you than I did our older sister. I felt we had always gotten along famously until I started to become ill.

One of the symptoms of the prodromal phase of schizophrenia was irritability. I would often lash out at you for annoying me. This usually happened when we were out and about.

I'd be strutting along, all full of myself, and then you would accidentally step on my trailing coat, making me stumble and look stupid (as I saw it back then). I'd get snappy with you and tell you to stand further away from me.

Often I'd feel guilty immediately after lashing out and try in a conniving way to talk you into being friends again. I pushed a lot of people away from me like this. The mixture of schizophrenia and being a teenager meant that I just couldn't cope well with people.

I now acknowledge that I've been ill for longer than I first recognised. When I was first medicated on Olanzapine, I thought I'd been ill for only two months. Those two months were the darkest parts of the psychosis, the time when the voices were at their worst, and when the delusions became most elaborate. But the psychosis phase was longer than I first realised, and the prodromal phase stretched back further in time than I knew. I do wonder if, in some ways, my whole life has been marked by this illness.

Sometimes at night, while I was young, I would feel a strange fear overtake me, even though nothing scary was happening. On one occasion the feeling hit me when I was playing with my dinosaurs. It was dark outside, and the light in my room seemed too bright. I suddenly felt afraid. So I went downstairs and told our dad that I'd scared myself while playing.

There were of course the hallucinations I had throughout my life. I seemed prone to getting them any time I had anything like a high temperature. I'd be seeing things like missing stairs, oversized spiders crawling over me, and the sofa tipped over when it wasn't. There was a particularly horrible one where the lampshade in our room would move up and down the wire connecting it the ceiling, the whole fixture moving closer and closer to where I lay in bed.

The spiders I used to see were caused by a sleeping medication I was on when I was very young, and spiders were to feature in my hallucinations for years after I stopped taking the medication. Sometimes I'd open my eyes and see an oversized spider running towards my face, dissolving away just before it hit my eyes. It was the fact that I was used to visual hallucinations that made it harder to identify I was getting ill with schizophrenia. When I saw things, I often just put them down to my usual condition.

When I was fifteen, I had what I term the fairy delusion. It occurred one day while I was in mum's living room, sitting on the sofa. I saw a small spider hanging from a strand of web in front of my face. Except I didn't see it as a spider but as a tiny fairy. The spider's back legs were her arms raised over her head, like a ballet dancer: the spider's front legs were the fairy's legs, and the four legs in between became her wings. I saw the spider's abdomen as her head. I was amazed. I was shocked, too, because seeing the fairy shattered my world-view. I wasn't ill enough yet not to be shocked that I was seeing fairies. Had I been deeply psychotic at the time I might have not thought much of it. But this time, after I stared a while in disbelief, reality reasserted itself and I realised I was looking at a spider.

Another delusional incident happened a couple of years later, when I was seventeen or eighteen. I'd had a coat made for me, and on the first day I wore it I damaged the corseting on the back in a small place. I was really upset about this at the time because of my concern for my image, and because the coat was new. The day afterwards, I woke up and went to put my coat on for school, and as I checked it over for the damage, I looked in the wrong place. I was amazed when I saw there was no damage, because clearly the coat had fixed itself, and I again felt shocked by this magical thing that had happened. My delusion evaporated when I realised I'd been looking in the wrong place for the damage. When I realised this I broke down and cried.

This was the nature of my delusions. At first they were brief, intermittent occurrences, which would manifest then disappear. As the illness progressed, they became more frequent and prolonged until they didn't go away.

I always take the beginning of my illness from being around age fifteen, even though I feel it has been woven through my entire life, even impacting on earlier parts. I count it as starting from age fifteen because it was around this time that my sleeping patterns got much worse.

After I was ill, I seem to recall you saying to me, "You thought you were the devil, didn't you?"

At the time, I nodded briefly in your direction, this was because at the time my story was too painful to tell. As you can see now, the real issues were much more complicated.

In the other letters in this collection, I have written about how I always felt a displacement from the human race, and felt as if I was non-human. I've written how I chose to see myself as a demon, because I liked demons. But I never, even when ill, thought I was the devil, or the Antichrist.

The reasons I felt close to the idea of being a demon also won't surprise anybody reading this. I felt like a devil, with my deceptive abilities and my hatred of humanity, and my inability to love anyone. I relished being terrifying, and hungered for power. There was also my ability to interpret human behaviour and use it to my advantage, which is something demons are said to do. My illness seemed like hell, and I had been cast out into it.

An important feature of my illness is that it didn't completely rob me of self-awareness. I have heard that many people with schizophrenia often don't talk to themselves in public, and this suggests that the type of awareness I had is not uncommon. It was as if I had a small sliver of sanity reminding me that if I spoke to myself in public I would be deemed mad. So I had enough awareness to appear almost normal on the outside and could appear to be functioning quite well.

I was lucky that grandiose delusions were not really something I suffered from. A grandiose delusion is the kind which makes the sufferer think they are a famous figure from history, or from mythology, or that they possess powers others do not. It was only really towards the end of my illness that I thought I might be imbued with telekinesis.

Delusions are beliefs without doubt. The delusions a person has are, I feel, exaggerations of the beliefs they'd hold when sane. For example, someone who is fascinated by politics might believe the voices they hear are the government spying on them through microchips implanted in their body. People who are Christian may believe the voices are angels or demons. Of course, this is a simplification. There are nuances to delusions, which tend to become more complex as time goes on.

For me, any legitimate belief always contains an element of doubt, and it is this which separates delusions from beliefs. Having an agnostic streak seemed to prevent me from thinking I was Satan. Instead, my delusion was a delusion of persecution. My experiences of being bullied made me believe it was bound to happen again. So, my voices took the form of students bullying me.

For all that my awareness meant I never became Satan, my desire to be evil and scary meant I wanted people to think I was him. I lived in a fantasy world which relied on the perceptions of others, and it made me excited to see that others were afraid of me. The voices realised this and tore me down. Every move I made, they were a step ahead of me. They even told me they were sent by Satan to punish me for my behaviour. I didn't believe them, replying "You hate Satan more than you hate me."

Becoming so deceptive made me feel internally guilty, and I wonder if the voices represented this guilt. I was like a spider weaving a web around me, ensnaring everything that came near, and consuming those who got to close. It is this awareness of myself and what I was doing which makes my story a hard one to tell. I have worn so many faces to so many different people that revealing my hand now becomes so very difficult.

Schizophrenia also causes a massive identity crisis. Afterwards, when under the influence of medication, you begin to wonder who you would have been without the illness. If not for schizophrenia, would I even be the same person? Would I still have been into Satanism, and had the same religious ideas? Or was everything a product of my illness?

I apologise for the times when I was weird, and for the times I treated you badly. One thing I didn't even consider was how my behaviour might have made people perceive you at school. It never even occurred to me that my behaviours might have consequences for others. Feeling as strongly as I did caused me not to care about anyone else or how they felt.

Letter to the Voices: Part Seven
Storthes Hall
Nov 2006- Jan 2007

Don't Look at the Canal

I wander from the doctors' door.
Gloom settles in.
Is there no help for a devil?

They are inside, not that I know.
Gloom settles in.
Don't look at the canal.

Back downstairs in my flat, I begged you yet again to come and talk to me, hoping we could discuss the situation like responsible adults. The cruellest of you shouted, "Attention seeking bitch. We should just ignore her". So that is what you did, and of all the experiences between us so far, I found this one the weirdest. You ignored me for four days (or what I felt was four days: my grasp of time was poor when I was ill, so perhaps it was simply one day that I believed was four).

People may think this respite from you would have made me calmer, but those days without you were just as torturous as the days filled with your abuse. I so badly wanted to contact you to clear up the mess I'd made that being ignored made me desperate. When I was in my flat, I spent the whole time begging you to come and talk to me.

I knew you were still there somewhere. Whenever I went into university, I'd be walking around thinking everyone was secretly laughing at me. I was so desperate to stop your character assassination of me, and your silence was so deafening. Not hearing you felt strange. I knew you were there watching me and judging me, sharing stories amongst yourselves, it's just that I couldn't hear what you were discussing. It wound me up to think that you could be saying anything about me and I just wouldn't know.

I felt so compelled to talk to you and get my point across that, while in my flat, I kept writing signs and putting them where you could see them. These signs were the only way I could contact you, because you were clearly still watching my room. To this day, I still have many of the signs I wrote to you.

Eventually you relented shouting "Okay, we'll talk to you again!"

"Attention seeking bitch."

Then my head was noisy again, and you were all chattering, talking about what I was doing.

To assuage my guilty feelings about all I believed I'd done I began writing in my books again, amidst the shouts of "Wanker!"

"She's pretending to write suicide notes."

"No! She's going to kill herself."

"She's writing plans against the human race."

Eventually I became so frustrated with your constant speculation that I ended up throwing my book across the room. It collided with a glass of water that was on top of my CD player, shattering the glass and killing the sea monkeys I'd been growing. However, because the book was black, and I was under the burning glow of my red light, I believed you hadn't seen me throw the book. And you hadn't.

All of a sudden came the shocked cry "She's psychic."

"Did you not see? She broke the glass with her mind."

You all became afraid of me, and once again, either because I never learn, or learned I couldn't win, I never told you that you were mistaken.

You started speaking of me with respect again, whispering.

All the while I could hear you talking amongst yourselves, "I thought she seemed to change her behaviour depending on what we were saying."

"How did she know?"

At all this whispered terror I broke down in laughter, doubled over, laughing manically at what you were saying. Then suddenly one of you roared, "She can hear us!"

Throughout the illness I'd heard you discussing my behaviour, and how I seemed to react to you even though I couldn't possibly know what you were saying. In my muddled confusion, it didn't occur to me that we'd been able to hear each other all along.

The revelation that you knew I could hear you felt like a culminating moment. This distortion of reality was much like the non-existent skylight, in that I couldn't perceive the plot holes in what was going on. Then my heart sank, as I heard you say, "We should spy on her all the time now to make sure she doesn't deceive us." I felt a black wave of despair wash over me. It was bad enough being spied on from time to time, but the idea that you were going to constantly watch me was horrific.

Up until this moment, the spying hadn't been constant. I knew you constantly talked about me, because I could hear you discussing the rumours that you created. But now I was also going to be kept an eye on all the time. I decided that I needed a shower and went to the shower cubicle in my room. I turned on the shower, got in and wept while sitting on the floor. All the while I could hear you gleefully saying, "She's trying to wash away the stench of failure."

I didn't want you to see me crying, because I knew I'd be mocked for it. During this time I'd also be careful to hide my periods from you, so you wouldn't laugh and mark me as human.

I felt a failure, I felt dirty, I felt that the situation had no end. Nothing I did could make the torture stop. Even apologising to you never worked. Begging you to come and speak to me only prompted cries of "Attention seeker!". You were all-pervasive, always present, watching me and prying into my life. There was no escape from you. It never occurred to me that things could get worse.

I got dressed and went back to the bed. I lay down, despairing, making sure to breathe as shallowly as possible. Then you started a new game. The game was scrutinising my facial expressions. If I looked angry, "Oh look she's pretending to be evil." If I looked sad, "She's going to cry now." If I managed to keep my face neutral, you'd shout, "Face bovvered!" at me.

Since I couldn't do anything right, I'd end up doing nothing except lie on the bed and try not to provoke you. From then on, if you interpreted my behaviour to mean something bad, I'd stop that behaviour. I became a phantom. I was hardly sleeping. I was hardly eating. I was doing nothing.

After weeks of this, of me lying around and doing nothing but listening to your taunts, I decided to make an appointment with the university doctor about my depression. I still didn't realise there was anything else wrong with me. I waited patiently for the day on which I could see the doctor, cheered by the thought that there might be a remedy for my low feelings, even if it meant you'd still be spying on me. At least I wouldn't have this terrible depression as well.

The walk to the university doctor took me alongside the canal. I can recall the day being crisp and bright, and I felt quite positive about taking steps to get help. The doctor's office was small and painted white, the décor softened with office plants. The doctor himself seemed compassionate and friendly. He asked me, "What seems to be the problem?"

I said, "I'm suffering with depression."

Then went on to explain that I was being bullied, and how the bullies were claiming my religion was faked, and that they were calling me an attention seeker. I think I may also have told him,

"They keep spying on me, and deliberately misunderstanding me."

I was devastated when the doctor said to me, "I think you are not clinically depressed, you are clinically pissed off."

He explained his assessment of the situation, which was straightforward: I was bound to feel upset when I was being treated the way I was. I left his office feeling despairing again. Having found no relief, I had nowhere else to turn and nothing I could do. I could still hear you mocking me, and tried hard to avert my eyes from the canal. I got the bus back to Storthes and trudged slowly back to my flat. I picked up my pen to write my thoughts into my books, your cries of, "She's pretending to write suicide notes!" making me feel angry and hateful. In my despair, I grabbed one of my canes and started whacking it into the roundabout bollard I used as a laundry hamper. I whacked it until the cane snapped.

Later in the week I went to the supermarket. I have no idea what I was going to buy, given that I barely ate anyway. During the walk from the bus to the supermarket I could hear you following me, making nasty comments. I passed a park and thought you must be hiding in there somewhere. When I finally got to the supermarket, I was upset to find you must have followed me inside. I could hear you commenting on what I was doing. As I went round carrying my basket, I felt hateful of humanity that you'd stoop so low as to follow me.

While walking round the supermarket I could feel your eyes upon me, but when I looked for you, you'd dart down the aisles so I couldn't identify who you were. I searched the aisles, but you always kept out of sight. In the end, after I'd paid for my shopping, I walked through the town centre feeling I was being followed and scrutinised.

WHAT IS this PAIN

A Letter to my Mum
Doncaster
1987-Present

To The Brutal

What can I say? You never gave way.
All of you should feel ashamed,
because it was always me you blamed.
For I was that bitch who stood up for myself,
not running away to protect myself.
I saw no reason to hang my head low,
no embarrassment set my cheeks aglow.
But you all used my reactions, to justify your decisions,
a simple attraction to hurting my ego.
I was spat at and hit, treated like shit,
yearning for a little bit of kindness.
I hope you find this true, I was bullied by all of you.
And very few of you, believed you were doing harm,
while I tried to remain calm, as the teachers let you off again,
all smarm and charm as you explained why I was pained.
"I only said one thing to her miss."
Not realising this, there were twenty of you, and me and my mate,
and that insults accumulate.
Like a dam which overflows and bursts,
I wish I could say my school years were the worst.
But your ire had an impact, a simple fact I cannot retract,
your words smacked, smashed into my future,
for when I became ill, my delusion began to fill in the pieces,
creating people who did the same to me, again, and again, and again.
With simple brutal remarks, I felt my world going dark, and was

reminded of you.
You oh the brutal, telling me I'm not beautiful,
telling me that I'm worthless, not perfect,
when it was all only projection, a moment of insurrection,
against yourself and against others you knew,
all your hatred grew and grew.
I wish I could say I'm past this now,
but I still remember every blow,
my mum says I should let it go,
but memories stay, and my memories stray,
and I'm stuck with torments that don't go away,
I have to live with this day by day.
While you the brutal sit and pray,
hoping the same thing won't happen to your children,
because the simple truth of the matter is,
one insult might just kill them.

While I was getting ill, and during my illness, I always regretted that I had a family. I was so determined not to be human that the fact I had earthly connections was embarrassing to me. I didn't want people to know I had mortal ties.

You, however, have always been there for me. It was important that you didn't see me in the same way that I saw you and my family relations. I really could not have survived without your care. As we both know, I was born with no hip socket. In my earliest years I couldn't walk. You made great efforts to make sure the doctors took you seriously and realised I wasn't just slightly delayed with walking. It was because of your efforts that they made me a hip socket using my own bone, cutting and twisting part of my pelvis to fabricate what others were born with.

When I did eventually learn to walk, I could do things most children could, although when I was tired I would walk with bit of a limp, and one of my legs remains slightly shorter than the other. Throughout my life I was bullied, and you had to put up with seeing me coming home crying after being attacked by my peers. Seeing your most sensitive child upset so much of the time must have been heart-breaking for you, and it must have been a massive fight to get the teachers to listen to you. You were always fighting for me.

I spent a lot of time hiding in my own inner world, probably as an escape from the bullying I often suffered. I had a big imagination and preferred my own company to the company of other people. Over the years I was in and out of hospital for various reasons. I had to have ear grommets fitted, and on another occasion I haemorrhaged from my nose and had to be rushed to hospital.

During secondary school, on top of the bullying I suffered there, I found that if I over-exerted myself my hip would hurt. I ended up in hospital on bed rest many times before the doctors realised I had a bone tumour. Fortunately, the tumour turned out to be benign, a bony growth that had developed on the inside of the hip joint. Despite this I did well in my school exams, although at the time I had hoped my grades would be higher, perhaps underestimating the adversity I'd faced.

The bullying I endured at school had a lot to do with the seemingly random nature of my hip problems. Because of this, I'd sometimes be in a wheelchair and sometimes not, and I would often be labelled an attention seeker, an accusation the voices later echoed.

There was a time, probably when I was about twelve or thirteen, when I was attacked after school. I'd had an argument with my main bully at the time, and she and her friends threatened to get me later. At the time I thought little of it, as bullies were always saying this sort of thing to me. But later, when I was heading home, a large group met me out in the quad. One of them shoved me and said, "And where do you think you're going?"

I replied "Home."

And then I had to fight my way through the crowd of pushing, shoving, sneering, people who were pulling at my clothes and hair. Someone grabbed my backpack to prevent my escape, and while I tried to struggle free a boy from my year laughed nastily in my face.

I pulled free and continued on through the mob. To get home I would have to go over the cross bridge across the main road, so I climbed the steps with the group in pursuit. They were jeering and trying to kick my legs from under me. I had to decide whether I should walk down the steps while people kicked me, which was dangerous, or whether to walk down the wheelchair ramp, which would take longer. Deciding on the shorter route I clung to the handrail tightly while people pushed, shoved and kicked me. The crowd only dispersed when they realised your car was waiting to pick me up. You told me at the time you'd wondered who was having a fight. You must have been saddened when you realised it was me at the centre of the throng.

School was a constant source of stress for me. People would spit at me and try and trip me up in the corridor. They'd hold doors closed when I was in my wheelchair. I was always being picked on by someone, whether it was people accusing me of faking my illness, or bullies who were upset that I'd stood up for myself when they were being horrible.

Another problem I had to contend with was one you may not have realised: when I was young, I used to have irrational phobias. One of my phobias was that the walls would move inwards of their own volition and crush me to death. The reason this phobia existed was because my older sister, not meaning any harm, once told me a scary story.

The story went that I was walking down a long, dimly lit corridor, and at the end there were three doors. My older sister bade me pick a door. I chose one, and she told me I'd entered a darkened room. Then the door slammed shut behind me, and that the walls steadily moved inwards and crushed me to death. I was probably about five or six at the time of this story.

After that I became afraid to go to the bathroom alone. I reasoned that as the bathroom was the smallest room in the house, I'd have less time to escape if the walls began to close in on me. Every night for a long time after this story I'd sleep facing the wall with my foot pressed against it to check it wasn't moving. This phobia eventually left me when I was seven.

As if this wasn't enough, I also had a phobia that my heart might stop in the night, an elaboration on the theme of death anxiety. Among my other phobias was the weird one of being scared that I'd be stabbed with a pencil. This was because one of our teachers had once told us that if a person gets stabbed with a pencil, a red line goes up their arm and into their heart and they die in five minutes.

I'm not sure what the teacher was doing telling the class a story like that. Perhaps she was scared there might be a student uprising, and that we'd be armed with pencils. But after that story I began to experience a horrifying recurring dream in which I was in the headteacher's office with only five minutes to live, and a clock counting down the minutes. The clock looked like a thermometer whose level dropped every time a minute elapsed. This phobia only left me after a boy in school got into a fight and really was stabbed with a pencil. He didn't die in five minutes, or anytime during our school years. He is probably still alive and well.

The fears I had as a child had an all-consuming quality. Once I had a terrifying thought in my head, I couldn't get it out. My last and worst phobia was with me until the age of twelve. It centred on a rare illness called fibrodysplasia ossificans progressiva, or FOP. FOP is a genetic disorder that causes random bone growth throughout the body, eventually leading to paralysis for the sufferer and then death. I first learned about this illness from a TV magazine in an article entitled, "I am Turning into Stone." I became scared that I'd somehow become ill with it, even though I knew it was a genetic illness.

The idea of being paralysed was terrifyingly real to me because of the sleep paralysis I often suffered. At night, when the fear would inevitably come, I'd psychosomatically feel I was stiffening up. I'd move my limbs to make sure I was still mobile.

I can't say why I had these all-consuming fears. In my mind I knew they were unlikely to happen, yet I worried and fretted over them. I do wonder if they manifested because of the bullying I suffered, my high level of anxiety given concrete form. I am surprised that I never ended up with OCD, instead of the schizophrenia I later became ill with. I have since learned that phobias can be part of the prodromal stage of schizophrenia. My phobias seemed to go away as I got older and armed myself with knowledge.

I never spoke to anyone about my phobias, not even Amy. It was almost as if I feared voicing them aloud as it would give them concrete form, which would in turn make them seem more scary.

You always encouraged me in my interests, taking me to singing lessons and praising my artwork. Of course, I kept it a secret for a long time that I was into Satanism. I was worried about what you might say, because I didn't want you to be worried about me, or panic that I was into something dangerous. You never batted an eyelid when I said I wanted to dress differently, though you did threaten to confiscate my Marilyn Manson CDs when I seemed too depressed or moody.

Parents' evenings at school made me nervous, because they were the one moment when my two worlds—the world of fantasy I'd built up amongst my peers, and the world you were familiar with— would collide. I was always afraid the teachers might say something to you or point out my odd behaviour. Everybody at school knew I was a Satanist, but no one at home knew, except for Rosie. I was also worried that the other kids might have told their parents about me, and that one of the parents would talk to you about my alarming behaviour.

It was this same separation of worlds that made me uncomfortable with you entering my bedroom, because I had books around which I thought you might notice. I eventually told you I was a Satanist after my first year of uni, during the summer holidays, when you asked why I was not going out with Al any more. At first, I didn't tell you why we had split, but I resolved that I'd tell you the truth if you should ask again. You asked again sooner than I expected, a whole five minutes afterwards. I was downstairs leaning on the kitchen counter when I told you.

"I've been hiding this since being thirteen" I said. I really meant fifteen, but always added the descent into Satanism onto the figure as well. "I'm a Satanist." I nearly collapsed after telling you, and felt shocked that the truth had come out at last. I couldn't explain my faith to you because my shock and relief were so great that I was nearly fainting. I'd bigged the moment of revelation up in my head so much that when it finally came, I was undone.

Another significant event while I was home from uni over the summer during my first year was an audio hallucination I had. It was not like the voices, in that I knew it was a hallucination;

this is what made it stand out. I was asleep in bed and on the verge of waking, I could hear beautiful, unearthly music. Then my perception of the music changed, and it became hellish and ugly. I found myself paralysed, trapped until I could move again. I remember going down the stairs and telling you I'd had an audio hallucination. This was unusual because I thought I'd never experienced one before.

I never really realised how much you had to deal with, and I never knew the sacrifices you made for me, even on top of the difficulties in your own life. You had an abusive boyfriend after your separation from my dad, and then you had to deal with him bullying me and my sisters. When I was in hospital you always visited me. You held down a full-time job as well as running the gymnastics club, which I also took part in, along with my sisters.

Being bullied by your boyfriend was a terrible experience. When he was round at ours, he would make up arbitrary rules, but would contribute nothing to the household. There were times when he would deprive me of sleep by playing extremely loud music early in the morning, all for my apparent crime of having woken him up on another occasion. The house was fraught with fights between me and him, or between him and my sisters.

Once, when he was arguing with me in my bedroom, he lunged at me and lifted me up by my throat. I didn't know where to turn, and this made me feel bitter towards you because you never knew how to put a stop to his behaviour. He told you it was us, the kids, making up stories to drive him away. This was all happening at the same time as I was being bullied at secondary school, so I had no escape.

He would often laugh at me and call me a wanker, complete with unpleasant hand gesture. It was his favourite word for me.

No wonder the voices called me a wanker too.

When we fought, he wouldn't let me do the sensible thing and walk away. He would hold doors shut and use his body to block my path around him. He would often seek out arguments, coming into my room to start a fight while you were in bed asleep.

He banned my friends from the house, even though they didn't want to come over anyway, as he was so awful to them when they stayed. He would belittle my artwork, calling it juvenile, or crude, and also was cruel about my school achievements, calling me a big fish in a little pond. He'd been educated at a private school, and clearly looked down at the state school in which I was being educated. He eventually left our lives after I was diagnosed with the schizophrenia, when you made him leave. I wished you'd ditched him sooner.

We have been through a lot together, you and I, but of course nothing prepared us for the paranoid schizophrenia, my worst hurdle to date.

Even though you felt exasperated with me at times, such as when I was constantly ringing you from university during my illness, telling you I was being bullied and repeating the childish things the voices had said about me, you did try to help. My constant swearing and angry, harsh language must have alarmed you, because normally I wasn't the type to spout expletives. You couldn't understand why I was so obsessive about the bullies, and why I couldn't just ignore them. It must have made you feel helpless, being so far away where you couldn't check in on me. You probably felt angry, too, that these people were wrecking my experience of university.

Frustrated, you'd ask me questions like, "Don't they ever sleep?"

"They go to bed after I'm asleep", I'd reply.

"Do they have nothing better to do?"

"I don't know."

I had nobody else to turn to. Even though I didn't want a family, I really needed my family. I figured that you had all the answers. I called you because I thought you'd be able to help me as you usually did.

It didn't help that my delusions were so banal. Had I been saying weird things like the government was spying on me, or aliens were tormenting me, we may have been able to get help sooner. But you couldn't see my deteriorating state, so you never realised my bullies were not real people.

One strange and intriguing characteristic of schizophrenia is that the voices will often instruct the sufferer not to tell people about them. They use plausible stories or threats to do this, telling the sufferer their mission as a spy is secret, or that they'll hurt them if they tell. This illness is adaptable and seems to make it as difficult as possible for the sufferer to realise that they are ill and seek treatment.

Whenever I was bullied, I was very open about it, and this didn't change when the voices bullied me. I always told people about it. This gives me cause to wonder whether schizophrenia always manifests in a way designed to avoid cure. It certainly has many twists and turns, presenting the sufferer with new possibilities to pave over its own contradictions. "How can I hear these people from so far away?" you will ask yourself. "Your ears must be really good" comes the answer. The sufferer is then never inclined to question the new narrative.

Another way in which the illness prolongs its existence is in making the sufferer resist treatment. Some people with schizophrenia believe they are being poisoned and will refuse to take medication. Others, like me, will think they don't need the medication because they are not ill. Still others may avoid medication to avoid blunting their unique experiences.

My voices never needed to use threats, because what I was telling people was perfectly normal. Who wouldn't believe me when I said a bunch of students was bullying me?

Remember when I was in your room talking to you, and I told you I thought the voices were people from another dimension? I was, in a roundabout way, trying to say that I thought the voices could be linked to demonic possession. I was trying my best not to alarm you with this theory. And, being in the early stages of recovery, I also didn't want to be locked up.

This illness is cruel. It knows everything the sufferer knows, and acts of its own accord. I have never felt self-hatred, but something in this illness hated me.

You were also there for me when, in 2011, I was diagnosed with Asperger's Syndrome. I was referred to a doctor to get this checked out because of certain things I'd been saying to my community nurse. I had explained some of my theories about the universe to my nurse, and spoken of my isolation from people. So we went to a five-hour long interview with the doctor, thinking that I might be on the cusp of having Asperger's. The doctor asked lots of questions about my past, and how I related to people, and what I would do in certain situations. At the end of the interview, he diagnosed me then and there. "You definitely have Asperger's." he said. I'd done some research beforehand, so I was unsurprised at this diagnosis.

I tend not to mention to people as much that I have Asperger's, because I've coped with it for so long without knowing about it. It's a diagnosis that feels rather too late for me to do much about. Whereas I tend to tell people about having schizophrenia because I feel it's helpful to share something of my story. I also want to be open because I feel it may help other people with the illness and inspire people who don't have it to be better allies.

Perhaps it's my own insecurity, but I suspect people might not believe me when I say I have two mental health problems. People seem to treat mental health differently to physical health, and I feel they are less believing when confronted with the notion that someone has two problems which they can't see. I hope that, if I dare to publish my book, the content doesn't alarm you too much. Please appreciate this is a hard story for me to tell, even to myself.

In the end schizophrenia was another thing we got through together, and you never abandoned me even when you realised the nature of the illness I have. You looked after me while I recovered, and tried your best to understand. Recovery from this illness is a slow process, one which I'm still going through. I was traumatised when I first came out of the nightmare, and I went through many bouts of depression. I also made mistakes, such as going back to uni again while I was still too ill. But you encouraged me to do what felt right for me.

I love you, Mum. I've never said this before because our relationship was always so much about my dependence on you. But you've given up a lot for me. I love you even though I sometimes don't understand the mistakes you made in your own life, the ones that naturally impacted upon me. For years I was too prideful to admit I needed my family, but even so, my family has been instrumental in my recovery. I am very fortunate to have people around me who have supported me with such love and loyalty. Not everyone is so lucky.

Letter to the Voices: Part Eight
Storthes Hall/ Madrid
February 2007

Escape

I need to get away from you, I cannot stay here in Hell Here listening any longer.
I'd hoped I'd be stronger, and able to cope with you.
But here I am running away, for days and days, from your awful gaze,
My expression glazed, like pottery, ready to shatter, as if what anyone says really matters.
Unaware that madness had taken me.

Fed up with being tortured day and night, I made a snap decision to go on the university art course trip to Madrid. For some reason the choice to do this made me feel extremely guilty, and I was worried about being able to afford it. Madrid was not a place I was particularly interested in visiting, but I just wanted an escape from the mental anguish.

I signed up for the trip at uni one day and brought the sign-up form back to my room to fill out. On seeing the form, you started accusing me of trying to run away. It had never occurred to me that you could read the tiny letters on a form from where I believed your window was.

The consensus among you was that I planned to go and live in Madrid, and your opinions ranged from, "She's trying to run away" to, "She's on a secret mission, she's the Antichrist." As usual, I'd hear you arguing about what the facts were. Those of you who believed I was running away threatened to use the internet to spread the story of what you believed I'd done so that I couldn't hide from my sins.

I had to listen to these theories day and night until the day I was going on the trip. When the day finally arrived, I went to meet the coach at four in the morning. I was awake anyway, having heard you speculating about me all night, and you were still discussing me as I left for the coach.

"You can't run away, bitch."

"She's obviously going to acquire something important for her mission."

"Wanker."

"We'll spread rumours about what she has done to us."

On the flight to Madrid, I was worried we might crash. I've always been nervous about plane travel, and now I could imagine your glee at my death. I was determined to make it back home safely to defeat you.

When we arrived in Madrid my head was mostly quiet. I'd hear the occasional 'English tourist' commenting on my dress sense, but nothing as bad as what you had been saying. The reason I didn't hear your voices in Madrid, at least not as the voices I was used to hearing, was because I didn't believe you were there. I knew you weren't in Madrid with me. It was the same when I went home to my mum's house. I'd still suffer the other terrible effects of schizophrenia, lack of sleep, lethargy, flat affect, but didn't hear your voices, because you weren't there. You couldn't be.

Of course, you were still there, which is why I'd hear the English tourists in Madrid saying things about me. I'm a monoglot, but had I been able to speak Spanish then I may have heard Spanish people commenting on me.

One strange emotion I had whilst ill, was that every time I

was away from you I wanted to be back amongst you. I yearned to go back to university to confront you. It was torture being around your voices, yet every time I went home from uni, and I couldn't hear you, my desire was to be back there fighting you. The only thing I can attribute this feeling to is wanting to win.

I have no memory of how we got from the airport to the hotel, but I was quite impressed that the hotel had a key card system to get into the hotel rooms. I'd never come across this before. Because I was very ill and not eating much, my immune system was compromised, so I came down with a cold and ended up having a lousy time. Madrid in February was far colder than I thought it might be, so I hadn't packed my warmest clothes.

I toured the art galleries with the other students. Unfortunately, with all that was going on back at university, I had not thought to learn any Spanish. I had thought, in my English ignorance, that Madrid would probably be a touristy place and that people there would speak a lot of English. I was wrong about that. This made it a problem when I wanted food because I couldn't understand menus or communicate with anyone. In the Prado Art Gallery, I sat on the floor by an Anselm Keifer painting, and was wordlessly told not to do this. The woman looking after that room in the gallery, unable to communicate with me, had to indicate in sign language that I wasn't supposed to sit on the floor.

In the Prado I saw real Dalí paintings, and paintings by Frida Kahlo. They were so much more vibrant than they'd seemed in books. I was amazed by some of the Dalís. They were a lot smaller than I had expected, but the fine detail was phenomenal.

I was not overly impressed with Madrid itself, though I did enjoy a walk around the park while I was there. On the walk I came across a statue of Lucifer falling from heaven. The accompanying teacher asked me who I thought it was and, thinking he meant the artist who had made the statue,

I hesitated. The tutor then proceeded to cajole me, thinking I hadn't known it was Lucifer, while I protested in an irritated manner.

I had the best coffee I've ever tasted in that park. It must have been freshly roasted, because I've never had one like it again. While I was ill, I drank rather too much coffee, which probably compounded my sleeping problems. I was so tired all the time, and coffee was the only way I could perk myself up.

One day I took a train to Toledo with some of the other students, which—with my poor sense of direction and lack of Spanish—I wouldn't have dared do alone. I loved the railway station at Madrid because it was filled with massive leafy plants, and a pool with turtles swimming in it. That day in Toledo was my favourite part of the trip. The town was like a medieval fortress, apparently built by different cultures. I loved the great stone buildings with massive wooden doors, and the winding, cobbled streets. Toledo is famous for sword making, and I bought a dagger while I was there.

I didn't make much of our free time, though, because I had very few people I was friends with and was afraid I might get lost if I went out in the evenings on my own. So I spent a lot of time in the hotel room, feeling ill and trying to get what sleep I could. I didn't have the courage to find my own way around. Finding my way is still something I have great difficulty with. I usually have someone escort me to places, because if something should change in the scenery when I'm walking somewhere alone, it gets me confused. I am easily overwhelmed by maps as well, perhaps due to the Asperger's. Even in my home town I sometimes find myself lost or confused about which way I should go.

The continental breakfast in the hotel was nice, though, and this was the most I'd eaten in a while. I'd have fruit and yoghurt and pain au chocolat, then cereal or toast. Towards the last day there I started feeling fed up with the fruit, and a little sick.

Feeling physically ill put a damper on the nicer parts of the trip, and being mentally ill as well left me underwhelmed by Madrid. I had the sense that it was not as stylistically interesting as London.

Constantly hanging over me was the fact I'd have to go back home and face your torments.

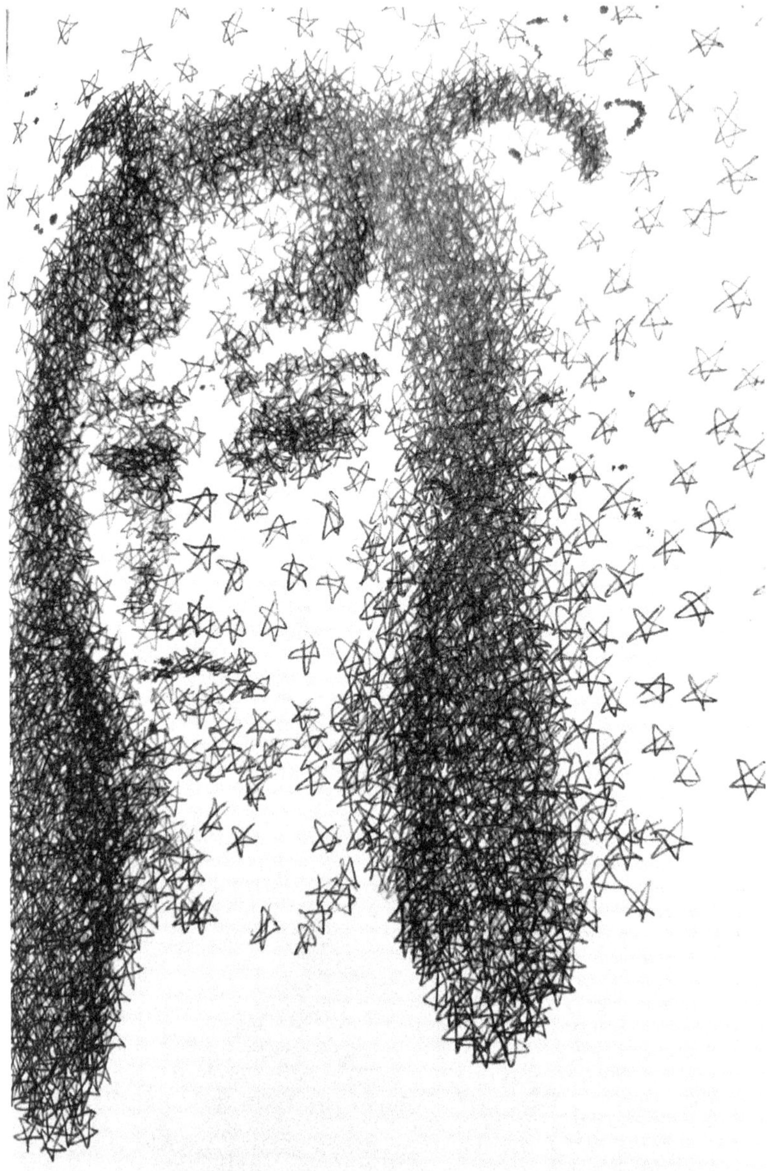

A Letter to Liz and Geoff
Doncaster
2012- Present

I Came Unplugged

Your tolerance hasn't wavered, since I met you there,
at this teashop telling you, and laying my illness bare.

I had no choice in this matter, at the time I didn't work,
I couldn't hide it anyway, not telling you just wouldn't work.

But you have always been there, taking me to places,
to singing groups, into pubs, and to meet new faces.

And even though my illness chases, we can make it work.

Ever since I met you and told you I have paranoid schizophrenia, you have been very accepting of me, even thanking me for being upfront about it. I understand it must have been a difficult thing to get your head around, especially since I was going out with your oldest son Rob.

I remember meeting you, Liz, while you were with your friend Christine. Rob had arranged for me to meet you at Woods Tea Rooms in Doncaster. I dressed in a long red and black netted skirt that looked like a princess skirt, a black shirt with a burgundy patent leather, underbust corset over it. I finished the outfit off with a fascinator with a small china teacup and saucer on it, to meet the theme of going to the tea rooms. I was nervous about meeting you but dressed the way I normally would because I wanted you to know what I was really like.

The discussion of what I did for work led me to tell you I was ill and at that time currently not in work. I always feel I had little choice but to tell people I was ill because some people, especially these days, do not understand why someone might not go to work. The question of what I did for work always made me feel a little bit awkward. I had no job, and people always asked this question, so I felt the need to explain my illness to them. Fortunately, you have always accepted me for who I am.

I read a statistic once, posted on Facebook by a mental health team called Rethink, that said only 8% of people with schizophrenia are in any kind of long term employment. This can partly be due to the symptoms. It's hard to seek work when the illness itself causes a massive lack of motivation, sleeping difficulties, and hallucinations. Add to this a fear of leaving the house alone because your reality has been upended and you have a formidable set of barriers. Another difficulty with finding employment is the stigma attached to schizophrenia. This means that sufferers are often looked upon as dangerous and a liability. At the very least, most employers prefer fit and healthy workers who will not need much time off.

I value the fact that you have both always loved me for who I am. You appreciate the love me and Rob share for one another, and you have always treated me as a daughter.

You have both been instrumental in getting me out of the house. With you I've enjoyed swimming sessions, afternoon tea, shopping trips, and visits to the pub, where Geoff and I have fun trying to outdo each other at the Doncaster Brewery Tap's unplugged singing sessions. I've been treated as perfectly normal by both of you, with no awkwardness around my mental health difficulties.

I've struggled with sharing the full nature of my experiences because they don't cast me in a good light. Having being a

Satanist makes sharing this story harder. This was something I wasn't ready to share, especially as it is such a misunderstood religion. I am not good at explaining it in person, partly because of having hidden it for so long from my mum, and I always get a Pavlovian response of awkwardness when I discuss it openly.

You have only seen me at my best, which makes it easier for you not to judge me. But even so it means a lot to me that you've never told me and Rob we couldn't be together. Since meeting Rob, my life and mental health have improved. Before that I was stuck indoors a lot, mostly at my mum's house, with only myself for company. My mum had to work, and usually came home exhausted from her physically demanding job, so she didn't have the energy to do much with me.

You have helped me more than you can imagine. I've enjoyed the various social occasions we have shared together, like our visits to the trolley bus museum and the holidays we've taken together. I've been to many more places than I'd ever seen before. I'm not good at researching places to go, so I never really know where I'd want to visit. But because you invite me along, I've now been to Bruges, and to Sweden with Rob to visit his friend. Even in Britain I've been to more places including Portland, Beverly, Cheshire, Aberystwyth, Edinburgh, and Liverpool for Rob's thirtieth. We've shared so many adventures together.

I still remember with joy your reaction when Rob and I announced our engagement to you. Liz jumped up so suddenly for a hug that the cat almost ended up on the ceiling. I couldn't ask for a better extended family, and I thank you for your tolerance and understanding.

Letter to the Voices: Part Nine
Storthes Hall
Feb – 2007

The Hanged Man

Round and round we go, like some macabre merry-go-round.
Deceiver.
That's what you call me.
It starts like this, with you spying on me,
you see the supernatural anomalies,
I, in order to restore my shattered dignity,
pretend you are right.
That you have seen the unusual, the mystical, the metaphysical.
Then you realise you are mistaken,
that there was no demon, no psychic shattering of glass, no fiery halo.
And then you call me a deceiver,
and I receive the blame for not having spoken up.
The blame you would attribute to me sooner,
had I have breathed a word in the first place.

When I returned to England on the plane from Madrid, I was dismayed to see that the country was blanketed in snow. I was upset about this because I was afraid I'd have snowballs chucked at me, being that everyone hated me.

Knowing you'd pick on me for being unwell with a cold, I decided that I'd wear a demon mask when travelling to and from university. These masks were the ones I'd made for the Team Satan project, but I often wore them. The only person I confided in that I had a cold was Kris.

As soon as I set foot on the Storthes Hall grounds I could hear the cries of, "She's back." I could hear you making owl noises at me, amongst other cruel taunts. Realising nothing had changed, I felt despair creep over me again. Back in my flat I could see snowballs being chucked at my window, but whether they were real or not I couldn't say.

Later in the evening the lack of sleep had made my eyes dry, so I filled my chalice with water and dipped my finger in, dropping droplets of water into my eyes, hoping to moisten them. Of course, you didn't let that one slip by. "She's pretending to cry for sympathy. The devious bitch."

"Liar."

"Kill yourself."

I found the anger rising within me again, and the frustration at your lies. It occurred to me that you didn't really believe the things you were saying about me. You were just pretending to believe them, hoping to spread convincing lies to the gullible. As I seethed with rage. I heard one of you say, "She's got a fiery halo around her head!" Once again, you all fell silent and started talking in that hushed way, that you did when your views had changed.

"See, I told you she was evil."

"She looks so angry."

"It's the devil's fire."

Then you reverted to fearing me once more. I knew in my heart that you were again mistaken, that my red light must be creating the effect. So I sat still, hoping not to break the illusion. I didn't turn around to check if there really was a red ring of light anywhere. I was unmoving, knowing that once this was over and you realised you were wrong again, that I would be tortured.

I sat there, I don't know how long for, until my eye landed on the shiny silver foil of a chocolate wrapper, with red light glinting off it. I wondered if you'd seen it and decided it must be this that was creating the halo. My efforts to avert my eyes from the chocolate wrapper alerted you to what I'd noticed. Once more came the cry, "The devious bitch!"

"She's tricked us again."

And "Face bovvered!" as I tried to look like you weren't upsetting me.

Inside I was distraught, and I knew I'd messed things up again. My desire to have you play my way was so strong. I wanted respect not aggravation. I had a feeling that I'd let down those of you who believed in my world, that you'd be disappointed in me for not being what you wanted me to be.

Eventually, after more long and arduous days, I requested that the university allow me to transfer my accommodation on the grounds of bullying. I can't fully remember the process, but I do recall my feelings of elation when it was granted. I would finally be able to move away from where you were spying on me.

stirred and drip served
fire The devils fire the [illegible]

the devils fire the devils fire
the devils fire the devils fire
the devils fire the devils fire

the devils fire
the devils fire

the devils fire the devils fire
the devils fire
the devils fire
the devils fire the devils fire

[illegible]

A Letter to the Students of Storthes Hall
Return to Huddersfield uni
2009-2010

I Wish I Hadn't Returned

I went back to what I knew.
Bored with recovery, lying about the house,
days lengthy, the only excitement being the delivery of letters.

But as is my fate, I got bullied again,
by, as usual, people who didn't understand me,
or know the road I've walked. But people talk.

People who didn't believe me when I said I'd suffered,
those who decided they knew more about my life than me.
Perhaps I should be tougher.

I needed understanding,
I wasn't very good at handling, your cruelty at this time.
People talk, and I walked away.
Leaving you to speculate on who I was in those days.

Recovery is boring.

After all the 'excitement' of being preyed upon by the voices, and of having to constantly fight for my sanity and survival, the aftermath just seemed dull and colourless. During this time, I was very apathetic, and it felt as if I had nothing to do, that nothing was happening, and that I had no reason at all to exist.

The medication, coupled with the damage to my senses from the illness, caused me to sleep a lot. I often wished I wouldn't wake up. I yearned for something to happen. Because I was always in the house, my mum tried to keep me socialised by taking me to salsa classes and made sure I stayed in touch with friends and family. At the time I felt unbothered about going out because I was constantly tired. I didn't realise that the wake of the illness would leave me so exhausted. I thought I was just being lazy when I slept all the time.

In January of 2009, I moved in with my friends Amy and Mark, which alleviated some of the boredom. We had a lot of parties while I lived there, celebrating our birthdays, our friends' birthdays, Halloween, and the New Year, which gave me things to plan. Often my friends would be around to talk to.

Still, while I lived there, I suffered bouts of depression and continued to sleep a lot. I had some of my weirdest hallucinations in that house, including a serpent lurking over my bed and a face made of swirling numbers. Though I had my friends to live with, I quickly became bored and was looking for change again. It was then that I decided I wanted to return to Huddersfield to restart my degree course.

This would be the third time I went to uni. I think of it as my second time, though, being that the brief return in September 2007 was to try and complete my third year. This time I would be starting over, re-entering the first year. I see now that I went back for entirely the wrong reasons. I wanted to recapture the spirit of myself that I felt I'd lost. I wanted an excuse to be able to dress extravagantly again, without feeling I would stand out too much, and I was looking to regain the charisma which had left me in recovery.

So I ended up returning to uni and living at Storthes Hall again, in another flat. This time I'd be living at the front of the complex, in a place that wasn't overlooked by other flats. The view from my window was the grassy lawn of Storthes and the woods. I was three storeys up again, which made me feel free to put my red light and HELL HERE sign back up.

I put my window sign up again because I suspected some of the students from my first time at university might be still around. I didn't want them questioning what had changed with me. So I dressed up in my gothic attire and swanned around the university as before, but this time I felt different. Gone was the bravado and charisma I once had. I felt a lot more awkward, and I worried about peoples' reactions to me.

I don't feel I came across as completely terrifying this time. After my illness I'd had my hair cut into a bob. I usually tend to prefer my hair long because it looks more ethereal, but I kept it shorter this time so I could wear my wigs. One of these was a long, straight, white-blond one. I wore my various styles of horns a lot as well but feel overall I came across more human.

The first time anyone saw me with horns on at uni this time round was when I was wearing them in my flat. I heard a person from outside comment, "Fucking hell." He then proceeded very earnestly to tell his friend that he thought I could be the devil. I was at first, in my usual way, proud of this, until I realised just how genuinely he seemed to believe it. Then I felt uncomfortable at the idea that maybe he was developing schizophrenia and perhaps I had just triggered a delusion in him.

I still listened to a lot of music, but not until three in the morning. I'd discovered some new music as well, so I'd listen to Emilie Autumn a lot, and to The Mighty Sieben, along with my usual classical music. In some ways, I did genuinely try and behave more normally than I had the first time at university. I tried to keep up my singing, which I hadn't previously, apart from when very ill.

The problem with my singing was that I used it as a way of showing that I was normal. I was hell bent on proving to an audience that I could sing. Which I clearly can, as I have grade eight in musical theatre. But this time, because I believed that everybody hated me, I'd feel underconfident. When I sang, I was very nervous and messed up quite a bit, particularly if I thought people could hear me or were watching me. My mistakes caused people, either real or imaginary, to laugh at me and say cruel things, which upset me. Still I kept up my singing, and sometimes it went badly, but at other times it went well. Ever since the voices tormented me, I've been excessively nervous when performing in front of an audience. The strange thing was that in the depths of my illness I could sing very well, despite the cruelty of the voices.

Something which didn't help during my university restart was a person, this time real, who kept ringing me up on the internal landline and saying insulting things. Out of boredom I sometimes went along with it, insulting him back. He was just another person looking for excitement at my expense, yet another person who couldn't cope with me being different.

He first called me on the phone claiming he was Satan, I hung up on him that time, and I feel he used this as reasoning to believe I was not telling the truth about my religion, as if I should have immediately believed that he was Satan. The thing about beliefs, particularly odd beliefs is people expect you to lack discernment, as if you should believe everything with no filter.

The person proceeded to keep calling up after that, I never worked out who he was except that I think he lived in a flat nearby. He was always rude to me and out of boredom I'd argue with him. I once mentioned that I didn't know why I bothered responding, and he said "Because you're lonely and desperate."

I just glared as I was used to doing forgetting he couldn't see me down the phone. On another occasion he called at five in the morning telling me I had a bad attitude, to which I responded "You've called me at five in the morning!"

He rang and pretended to be the TV licencing company at one in the morning, I paused wondering what to say, whether to point out that I did not have a TV or to point that TV licencing wouldn't ring at one AM. I decided to go for the latter, then he hung up.

I think it was largely because of this bully that people started saying I was an attention seeker and that I wasn't really a Satanist. As I still was at this point.

I'm aware some of the things I was getting bullied for, mirrored what the voices used to say, and this caused people back at home to think that I was suffering with the schizophrenia. And though I know the schizophrenia still had an impact, I don't think everything that happened to me this second time at university was my illness, though it is hard to tell.

I was still hearing some voices and had feelings of paranoia, which didn't help. My paranoia still centred around people hating me. I'd hear people referring to me as an attention seeker because of the way I was dressed. I was also preoccupied with the idea that another Student Room thread had been set up about me. I'd asked my friend to delete the one I'd made when I was ill, but the impression I now got from hearing you students talk about me, was that someone had set up a new thread and had pretended I was involved in it. This suspicion was exacerbated when I heard someone yell, "Attention seeker." at my window, and another person shouted back, "She's been set up." Whether these shouts were real or not I don't know, but they were enough to make me feel that you hated me.

The problem with this illness is that even in recovery I cannot entirely trust my senses. The things that happened during my last time at uni may not have been real, but to me they were. Yet

I don't know for sure. This is the reality I must live with. I never know for sure whether what I've seen was real. I often have to ask my husband, "Did I see that?" or "Did you hear this?". It puts me in a very vulnerable position. If something real and unwanted does happen to me, how am I supposed to prove it?

My behaviour during this period was a mixture of trying to be normal and trying to be true to the things I liked and enjoyed. Two years into my recovery, I really wasn't sure about my identity. Was I the Satanic girl from before? Or was I some new person who was doomed to feel lost? Having realised how much of my former behaviour was due to schizophrenia, I was filled with uncertainty.

To make matters even more complicated, there also seemed to be some debate on campus centred on whether I was telling the truth about my illness, because some people hadn't believed me when I came out and said it. Some assumed that because of my gothic predilections I thought it was cool to pretend to be mentally ill.

I recall a time when I was showing a friend some of my artwork on the bus, and I was explaining my illness, because my artwork was about that. I heard a girl on the bus say to her friend "Is that true?". Her friend replied that she thought I was lying, because if it were true I wouldn't just come out and say it.

Having people doubt me when I'd found the courage to be open was irritating and alienating, and I was angered by the implication that mental illness was something which shouldn't be mentioned. Although I feel shame over the things I thought and did while ill, the fact that I am ill doesn't shame me. I believe that more people should talk about their mental health struggles, because then it would become normalised.

I did have one good friend around this time, a girl called Sophie who lived next door to me. When I first met her, I didn't think we would get on. She seemed the type who'd be popular, and who wouldn't like me. She was always made up, with tidy hair, and seemed the complete opposite of me. But she happened to be studying psychology, and we got talking because of my illness. She found my stories about what it was like to have schizophrenia fascinating. Of course, I never told her all the gritty details about what happened to me. She was kind and stood up for me, even when others were less than friendly.

There were also a few students who asked me if I'd be a model for their photo shoot for their photography course, and it was nice to feel that some people accepted me. But I had trouble socialising and getting out of my flat. Eventually, exhausted by my own fear and the bullying, I decided to pack up and leave, still without a degree.

Letter to the Voices: Part Ten
Storthes Hall
Feb 2007

The Hermit

Locked in my room, with a vague sense of doom.
I can't come out of this place, for I have been disgraced.
I can't face them and their rumours, voices I hear in their countless numbers.
So I sit here in Hell Here, a hermit of my own making.

Relieved at the prospect of living beyond the reach of your critical gaze, my bullies, I started moving all my stuff into my new place. I'd enlisted the help of Kris, because over the course of my years at uni—having discovered the Huddersfield Saturday antiques market—I'd accumulated a lot of belongings.

We moved my large Athena print of William Blake's painting of God punishing Adam, my ramheaded lectern, all my CDs and books (none of which were boxed up), my bedding, my art supplies and folders, my picture of Lucifer, and many other diverse treasures. I was scared when it came to moving my art supplies, because I had a habit of rescuing things from skips on the university campus. Before I was accused of being a sheep shagger, I'd taken a load of white, synthetic, woolly material from a skip, with the intent of using it for my artwork. It resided under my desk in clumps, and I was afraid of what you might say on seeing these chunks of wool-like material.

In my attempts to convince Kris that I was actually being bullied, and that I wasn't insane, we had a falling out. I can't recall the entire content of the fight, but I remember telling him that the reason I could hear you and that he couldn't was that my ears were more sensitive than his. He was a music tech student, and my theory was that he couldn't hear you because he'd damaged his hearing by blasting music through his headphones. Kris nearly left then and there, but I managed to talk him back round. I still needed help moving my things. It had taken most of the day already, and on my own it would take ages.

When I finally got settled in, I decided not to advertise my presence. I didn't put up my HELL HERE sign, or use a red light. I didn't use any light, for that matter. The problem with this was when it got dark, I had to sit and do nothing because there was not enough light for me to see by. I also put a large art canvas in front of the window to stop anyone looking into my room. It didn't reach all the way to the top of my window, but it would do.

Despite my efforts you knew I was there, though, and the bullying got worse.

In my deluded state, I now thought I'd unwittingly moved to where the nastiest of you lived when he was not visiting his friends. He'd found out where my new flat was, and you'd changed your tactics: this time round, his friends would come to visit him, and you were all continuing to spy on me from his place.

At first I couldn't figure out where you were spying on me from. I was four storeys up in an L-shaped building, near the inner bend of the L, so there were flats overlooking mine quite closely now. For a while I thought you might be living in one of the overlooking flats, on a floor below my level. But one day you mockingly told me to look up, when I was looking for you out of the window. I realised you must live at the same height as my flat, and must be able to see me closely now. It was around this time that you started issuing physical threats, such as, "If I see her out, I'm going to punch her." These more violent messages made me afraid, and I started wondering if I should carry a knife with me for protection.

You had always kept your names secret from me so I couldn't report you to the authorities, but one day you slipped up while debating about me. You were all at my end of Storthes now, and had worked out which flat I lived in. You were saying the usual cruel rubbish about me.

Then the nicest of you said, "She's a genius."

Then another of you responded with, "Liam only says that because he fancies her."

Other than Adam, Liam was the only one of you whose name I found out.

I was elated that I'd found out a name because this might help me find a way to contact you. That night, to annoy me, you started shining laser pens into my flat. The canvas I'd put in front of my window didn't cover the top of it, and I could see large circles of red light dancing on my ceiling.

The circles of light had a diffuse appearance, so I knew they were being shone from the ground upwards. It never occurred to me that laser pen light doesn't diffuse that much.

At night I'd keep my lights off and not even use a torch, hoping you wouldn't be able to see me. I'd sit or lie in the dark doing nothing, huddled under my picture of Lucifer and trying not to move or breathe too deeply. Though extreme, my attempts to find some privacy didn't ever work.

You still found ways to aggravate me.

"Fucking freak."

"Wanker"

"She's going to cry now."

During the night if I had to do anything it would be done in darkness. This made you debate whether I could see in the dark, and whether this ability meant I was evil.

Another factor of my existence that changed drastically around this time was that I stopped singing. I was too pained and ill.

During the daytime I played music, but it was only to try and convey to you how I felt. If I felt the lyrics spoke of my situation, I'd play the music. During the music most of you would abuse me, but Liam would say what a genius I was, because I was clearly choosing the music to convey a message. On one particular day I heard a rumbling sound, and Liam suggested I was creating a storm with my mind. I assumed the sound was the bin men putting the big, communal bins away. But Liam continued to be enthralled by his idea, while the others of you said I was clearly playing a prank.

I hoped you wouldn't realise that the sound was being made by the bin men, because I knew you'd blame me for Liam's excitement. Which of course is exactly what happened. I didn't realise, in my woeful state, that there was no logic to you blaming me for the bin men moving the bins, but of course you did. I felt I'd deceived you again for not having told you. It was sheer torture that, even with the curtains closed and a canvas at the window, you could still see into my flat. You'd discuss me constantly as you were wont to do.

Another bizarre thing that started happening around this time was that I'd look at objects and see them jolt to one side. This made me wonder if I had telekinetic powers, and I'd whisper to myself, "What is happening?"

"Why is this happening?"

I also started to accurately predict what you might say to me, which comes as no surprise because we were so closely entwined. But because you'd so often say what I predicted you would, I began to think I might have powerful psychic powers.

Whenever I lay down to rest, I'd curl into a protective ball that hid my face, because you were still scrutinising my facial expressions. Eventually one evening I became so upset that I hid under my desk. Yet somehow this didn't stop you from seeing me. I believed you could see me through the hole that was cut into the desk for laptop wires to run down to the plug socket.

I called my mum, one of many calls I'd been making home, though I can't recall any of them except this one. I told her, "I'm hiding under my desk to stop them seeing me." My mum was extremely exasperated with me, since she didn't know the half of what I was going through. "Well why don't you call the police if you're so upset." she snapped. So after that phone call I decided to venture out to the security desk, where I angrily asked them if they knew the number for the police. One of the managers of Storthes Hall happened to be there at the time, and he said incredulously, "You don't know the number for the police?"

But I obtained the number from the security staff, and duly called the police.

anity is not statistical sanity is not
sanity is not statistical sanity is
sanity is not statistical sa
statistical sanity is not statisti
is not statistical sanity is not st
sanity is not statistical sanity is no
sanity is not sanity is
stical sanity is not statistical
statistical is not
anity is not statistical sanity
tistical sanity is not statistical
not statistical sanity is n
ical sanity is not statistical.
ot statistical san is not
sanity is not st
tical sanity

A Letter to the Policeman
Storthes Hall
28th Feb 2007

The Devil

That is what I perceived, what I should be.
I want to be no angel,
and human beings pale in comparison,
and I feel such a raging passion.

I fell over and over, into hatred,
into Hell.
A monster you made me.
A monster I made myself.

You came the day after I'd called to report that I was being harassed and that people were spying on me. I was so happy that I was finally going to get the situation sorted out. The whole thing must have seemed odd to you. And on this day for many years afterwards I would feel ashamed and embarrassed by our encounter.

You entered my room, which was a mess. The bed was unmade, the curtains were shut, with the canvas leaning against them, and there were art supplies scattered all over the floor. I said to you in a strange bout of self-awareness, "Sorry about the mess. It looks a bit like a schizophrenic's bedroom."

I was referring to the blocked-off windows, knowing from my psychology lessons at school that people with schizophrenia think they're being spied on. At this point I didn't have the insight into my condition to realise I was very ill.

I was trying hard to explain to you what was going on. At the same time, I felt the need to show enough bravado and arrogance to prove to the voices that they weren't getting to me. I explained to you that I was a Satanist, and that I was a self-styled demon. I repeated this many times, and I told you I was being bullied and spied on by students near my flat.

You were polite and courteous to me, but you must have found the whole situation hard to deal with. It was almost impossible for me to get my story straight while the voices were howling in my head. They pointed out to me, while you and I were talking, that I'd forgotten to change my underwear that morning.

Unfortunately, your response to my account was that without the perpetrator's names you could effectively do nothing. You advised me to find some like-minded individuals who shared the same interests as me and who could support me.

"Liam" I said suddenly, "I know one of them is called Liam."

But you told me that without a full name there was not much you could do. The voices were howling with laughter and saying they were off the hook.

"Have a nice day!" you said to me as you turned to leave.

I suddenly realised something at that moment, and said in a thin voice, "Oh… it's my birthday."

I'd totally forgotten that this day was my twentieth birthday.

You left, and I was left on my own with the voices. Then I called my mum at work and told her

"I'm coming home." She decided to pick me up later that night, and to take Kris and me out for a celebratory meal.

A Letter to a Lucky Survivor
Huddersfield University
28th Feb 2007

Your Vile Mirth

You laughed, and I grasped my cane,
hoping to end your days.
I was at the end of my tether,
destroyed and broken, willing to break others.

I was constructed of glass and heard your words,
heard words at least.
This was your rope, not mine this time,
your vile mirth was the end of the line.

You don' t realise how lucky you are, do you? To you this was a perfectly ordinary day. You probably were not even fully aware of me and have probably forgotten this incident.

I'd decided to go into uni on the day of my birthday, after the policeman had visited. I was walking along by the side of one of the buildings near the university shop. I was swaggering along trying to create an appearance of normality, to show the voices in my head that they weren't getting to me, when I saw you crossing the path ahead of me. Upon spotting me, you turned to your friend and said, "You'll never guess what she did," and grinned maliciously at me.

You walked past, and I felt an extreme rage. I assumed that you were implying I was a sheep shagger.

I don't know whether you really said this, but it's what I heard and saw. In hindsight this often happened when I was ill. Schizophrenia caused me to hear and see different things to what was actually said and done.

The day was a bright, sunny one, and I felt a terrible turmoil. I stopped and gripped my cane, which had a large pewter dragon on top. It came to me that I should follow you, and approach you from behind to smash you on the head with it. I imagined shouting at you that I wasn't a sheep shagger while hitting you repeatedly.

I was so frustrated that I wanted to cave your blonde head in to retaliate for what you had said. Fortunately for us both, a huge wave of depression hit me before I could start to follow you. Feeling ashamed and defeated, I walked the other way to catch the bus back to Storthes Hall, without even bothering to go into the art room.

Letter to the Voices: Part Eleven
Doncaster
Feb 2007- March 2007

Taketh Away my Bliss

I despise the human race.
I find they are a big disgrace.
Such disgust I feel.
Such contempt.
Whose minds I loathe.
Whose souls I steal.
I grieve of your ignorance.
You who make me empty.
You who made me hate.
I want not your lies.
Such careful scrutiny.
Such well observed 'evidence.'
Put together with the practised air,
of a child's jigsaw puzzle.
What about me?
Can you not hear me?
Can you not believe me?
Can you not feel my pain?
I want to give you pain for this!
You that taketh away my bliss.

Later that day, my mum came to collect me as planned. We picked Kris up and drove to an Italian restaurant, because I'd fancied Italian food. When I got there, however, the pizza and pasta didn't appeal. So I ordered the duck in orange sauce, though I couldn't eat much because I was convinced you had followed me to the restaurant. I could hear you saying that I fancied Kris and laughing at me.

In the restaurant I felt that I could risk going to the toilet. I'd been avoiding going in my flat, for fear that you'd laugh at me and treat me harshly. I was very constipated and, thinking you had followed me, I tried to be as quick as possible. I didn't get much relief.

Looking back, everything you said was juvenile in content, but I was robbed of the necessary sanity to cope, and it all seemed horrific to me. Your abuse was chosen from the playbook for the primary school bully: sheep shagger, toilet habits, sexual slurs, who I might fancy. All of it was the stuff of the playground but given an edge because I thought you were real, and that everyone believed your lies. The torture was constant and inescapable.

So I left uni, and at home I felt a little better and more hopeful. I couldn't hear you, but I still couldn't sleep and felt constantly sick at the rumours I imagined must be proliferating about me in the world. In the end, though, I decided I couldn't let you win. I resolved to complete my third year, but that this time I'd get a student house instead of staying at Storthes. I planned with Kris to find a house for us to share.

I went back to Storthes, to stay the night at Kris's flat so that we could attend the viewings we'd booked for the next morning. I'm sure Kris must have been upset by my behaviour, because I acted insane while I was at his place. I babbled about making a crown of animal bones, and wondered where I could find some. "Where do you think we'd find an abattoir for some bones?"

I kept asking.

I was dismayed when you shouted, "The abattoir! She got the dead sheep from the abattoir."

I could hear you talking about me, laughing cruelly.

"Fucked-up bitch."

I didn't sleep at all that night.

The next day we had three houses to view. Kris drove us around to see them, which took a large chunk of the day. I could hear you following me around whenever we were outside the car. We decided on a house and prepared to sign up as tenants.

Later on, I went back to the train station to catch my train home. I got on the train from Huddersfield to Sheffield so I could make the connection from Sheffield to Doncaster. I was disgusted to find that you were on the train with me. I could hear you discussing the rumours about me, and I ended up in tears on the ride home. I was on one of the seats facing sideways, and an old man was sitting near me on a forward-facing seat. I wondered if he might talk to me, but he didn't say anything, and I remember feeling affronted that he hadn't even asked why I was crying.

Then, to my further dismay, you started gloating and telling me I'd missed my stop. I panicked and hastily got off the train, leaving my bag of clothes on board. You were of course quick to point out that I'd left my bag behind, and I fretted, feeling despairing and stupid.

DCLXVI

ny me wh

why me

why me why me why me why me

e why me why me why me

e why me why me why me

e why me why me why me

e why me why me

e why me why me

e why me why me why me

e why me why me why me

e why me why me why me

e why me why me why me

e why me why me

e why

ny me why one why me

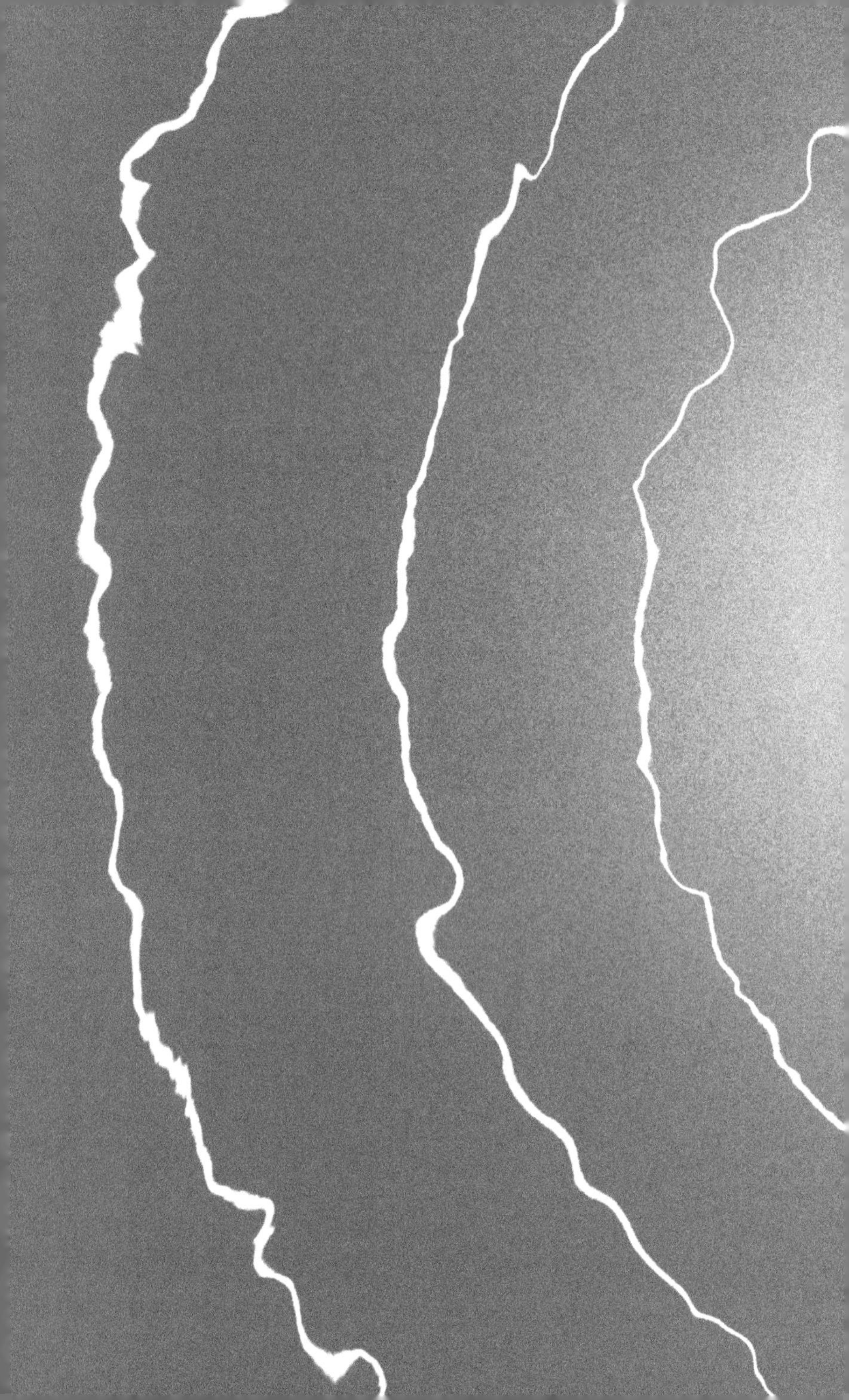

Part Three

Recovery

A Letter to a Helpful Stranger
Sheffield
March 2007

Kindness

Stranded and alone, stuck on that platform, shouting down my phone, help me out please!
Lost belongings, left behind, lost myself then a stranger so kind, helped me on that day.
Did he know I was mad? That I was hearing voices, who told me I was bad?
That I'd missed my stop so went and got off, stranded on the platform.

A stranger helped me on that day, while I was drowning, while I cried, and while I was frowning.
Who were you that put me on the right track, accompanied me and had my back?
Did I even thank you? Before I slunk off into that distance...

I still remember what I was wearing on that day: a red suit with a black shirt and black shoes. I had my claws on, I was carrying a cane, and I was wearing my inverted cross. The reason I remember what I had on was because the bag I'd left on the train contained my black suit.

You saw me while I was stranded on the platform near the waiting area, one stop away from Sheffield. I thought I was lost, and I didn't realise that Sheffield was the terminating stop, so I thought I'd passed it. Realising that I'd left my bag on the train, I was talking to myself saying, "Oh shit, oh shit," over and over.

I remember a young woman and her child sitting on the bench of the waiting area, looking at me strangely. I whipped out my phone and called my mum, telling her about my predicament. "Pull yourself together, ask a train guard where you are!" she shouted.

Sobbing, I hung up and went to find help, which is when our paths crossed. You were the train guard, and you could see I was terribly distressed. I explained to you that I was lost, and that I'd left my bag on the previous train. You told me I was only one stop away and let me know that the train I'd been on terminated in Sheffield. You offered to call ahead to the driver and get him to keep an eye out for my bag. I was in such a state that this only made me feel ever so slightly better.

You were kind, and even came with me on the next train to Sheffield, making sure I got on the right one. While I stood on the train next to you, I kept babbling to you that I was being bullied at university, and that I was being spied on. I kept bursting into tears and must have looked extremely distressed. I will never know if you were aware that I was extremely ill, whether you had been in that sort of position yourself, or if you knew someone else who had. Or perhaps you were simply an incredibly kind person. It felt so good to have someone show me some kindness.

After we arrived in Sheffield you escorted me to the lost property department to retrieve my bag. I can't remember if I even thanked you, but your kindness, coming while I was in such a dark place, is something I appreciate to this day. My general mistrust of people, the legacy of being bullied and attacked by real people and by the voices, means I struggle to be kind in the way that you were to me. I find it very hard to make small talk with people, and I fear approaching people to help them. But you inspire me to be helpful to others, because I remember how despairing I felt that day, and how your kindness gave me a sense of hope.

Letter to the Voices: Part Twelve
Doncaster
Mar 2007

Symptoms

Let's start with, I see things that are not there. I hear THEM. The outer demons, suffer delusions,
turbulent emotions, no emotions at times, outer demons punishment for my crimes.
Lack of motivation, word salad THEM again! Fatigue, lack of sleep, paranoia, outer demons,
irritation, impulsiveness, THEM reminding me of my selfishness. Guilt, guilt, guilt, a constant companion, emotions so strong they are painful, THEM, the outer
demons THEM the outer demons!

I was now hearing you in my mum's house in Doncaster, which had previously been beyond your influence. I started believing that you must have a flat nearby, and, from things you had been saying, it came to me that you had been watching me even before I went to university. I became convinced that you were spying on me from a tower block at the end of our road, and that you were using binoculars to see me. There was no tower block, of course. It existed only in my mind, to explain why you could see me in both sides of my house. Just as with the non-existent skylight in the art room at uni, whenever I'd walk to the end of our road, I once again found myself confronted with the fact that there was no tower block, only a small supermarket. Things got so dark and stressful for me around this time that I'd hit and scratch myself. My mum thought I was just sleep deprived.

She realised something was badly amiss one day while she was on the phone, standing in the hallway and talking. I was lying on the floor in our living room, and in my muddled confusion I forgot she was out there. I started ranting in loud whispers and getting angry with you. You had started talking about turning the tables on me, threatening to call the police over what you perceived I'd done to you, which naturally got me very scared. I was so embarrassed when mum came back in and asked what I was doing. I felt ashamed that she had heard me talking to you. It was as if part of me deep within knew you weren't real.

The next thing I remember was my mum saying she had booked a doctor's appointment for me.

"I'm not mad," I'd say to her, "They are trying to make me look mad, but I'm not."

You started tormenting me with a new game. You'd say, "She's got schizophrenia, she's so paranoid."

"No, I don't." I'd respond angrily. "It's you that's making me paranoid."

Upset about being spied on, I got my mum to cover my bedroom window with newspaper, but you could still see me. Even with the newspaper covering the window and the blinds drawn you could still see in. I kept thinking the newspaper must have fallen down behind the blind, but every time I checked it was still in place. I could hear you wherever I went, and the lines blurred between there being five or seven of you.

I have no recollection of visiting the doctor. I only know I went because my mum mentioned she'd taken me. Life was the darkest it had ever been for me around this time. I was in complete mental anguish. I'd see visual hallucinations, and you continued to torture me. You even watched me in the bath. I'd try and ignore you by blowing on the bath foam and watching the patterns it made. I wanted to drown.

All the things that happened around this time get very muddled up in my mind. Even though I try, I can't remember them clearly. One night when I was in the kitchen and you were verbally attacking me, I pulled a sharp knife out of the knife block and started brandishing it, trying in vain to scare you.

You accused my mum of being a drug dealer when she showed me a £50 note she'd made at the car boot sale, which of course added fuel to your accusations that I was taking drugs.

In my room one night I created an elaborate construction out of sheets and the long cords from some old tracksuit bottoms. I tied the ropes onto the light fitting to hold the sheets in a cocoonlike structure around the top of my canopy bed so I could hide from you. I still believed you could see me because the newspaper over the window had fallen down or had some sort of gap in it.

You even tried to blackmail me. I'd removed a sheet of the protective newspaper and was looking out of my window, trying to spot where you were. I looked out of the window to the house at the back of my mum's, wondering if you perhaps lived there. Then I hallucinated that I could see a young boy in the shower in that house. Thinking I was intruding on someone's privacy, I put the paper back up at the window and stopped looking for you. But then you started the rumour that I was a paedophile because I'd seen the boy.

You then threatened to spread the rumour that I was a paedophile if I didn't confess to being a sheep shagger. I was livid and tried to tell my mum what you had been saying about me. I must have explained it in the wrong way, though, because for a second, she went white and asked me,

"You're not a paedophile, are you?"

Mum asked this because she believed I was feeling guilty about something, and that was the reason I couldn't sleep. I was frustrated and became angry and tried to explain that I was being blackmailed by you. Despite my very real fear that you'd start this new rumour, I never caved into you. I knew that whatever I did or said you'd find a way to use it against me.

Face of Hatred

A Letter to the Party
Doncaster/ London
Sept 2023- Present

Taking Out Satan's Teeth

From fifteen I have trodden this path,
feeling connected, to what I've often seen,
as an evil entity.
I've twisted my mind in knots,
trying to justify, why?
It made sense when I was younger,
when I hungered for power,
and described a chill, a certain thrill,
from being connected to Satan.
But so much doesn't fit, as I become more benign,
in my older years, I rather incline,
to being a much nicer person.
God could not save me,
but Karl Marx can,
perhaps in a way I do not understand.
The only way I can exist this way,
is to twist Satan from evil to good,
and I don't think I should.
Taking out Satan's teeth seems irrelevant,
a pretence,
for if he is rendered safe,
then why not follow a different path?
It makes more sense in that case to worship a god,
or some benevolent force,
for of course, I still have beliefs,

and taking Satan's teeth,
may not change his nature.
Not that I'd like to become a preacher,
but I'd rather not feature such confusion,
it worked well when I was having delusions,
but I think I'm moving in a different way.
As the bell tolls, the snakes relax their hold,
and I begin to wander further,
but I don't know where to go.

It was a frigid morning in London that day in January. I was passing out leaflets for the party at the pro Palestinian rally, we'd set up our stall across the road from the river Thames, and the march was proceeding past. I never in my life could I have predicted that I'd become a communist and had been trying to decide whether to pursue this course for quite a while.

The difficulty I was having at the time was that I realised my opinions were shifting, I started seeing my belief in Satanism as a bit crude particularly considering the politics of Satanism. I'd been listening to Alexander McKay's political podcasts for about three years before the tipping point. I enjoyed Alex's grasp of history and analysis of what was going on in the world. As I slowly started becoming more politically aware I started realising the shortcomings of my religion. I'd been grappling with the notion of myself as Satanic ever since being a Satanist, I knew in my heart I wasn't a bad person and knew my agnostic Satanism made very little sense. I could not pin down what I really believed and often relied on my theories.

I'd say to myself that I believed in the possibility of this or that, which was true, but it was never a very concrete stance. The fact that I believed in the possibility of Satan existing made my agnostic stance particularly difficult, because what if he did exist and I was cast into hell? A hell that I never truly believed in, but believed in the possibility of.

I feel my turning to communism happened very slowly on the one hand, the tipping point however came very quickly, I'd find myself thinking over the things Alex had said on his livestreams while I was cleaning the school, and I'd imagine telling other people about what he'd said.

I'd also been reading Karl Marx's Capital, a lengthy set of books about how the working class is exploited by the capitalist class, it opened my eyes to my own conditions.

I'd beaten myself up many a time, while I was recovering from the illness, getting myself upset about why I was not achieving the goal of being an artist, and being able to make a successful career out of it. I realise now that the lack of social mobility for the poor is baked into the system of capitalism. I didn't have much money to set up any type of business, or have what Marx calls the means of production, which are the machines to produce things quickly, or some dedicated building to produce my work in. I simply had no money for these things.

At the time I was trapped in the benefits system, I had no job, and lived at home with my mum, I hadn't achieved any of the things on capitalisms list of success, such as having my own home, a car, a job, a relationship or children. So I used to worry, mostly about my job status, since the environment was very hostile to those who couldn't work, and still is even now.

While I cleaned the school I started grappling with my religion, I'd realised that I wanted to join the party and wondered could I reconcile my religion with it. I could feel I was on the brink of something.

One day I came home to my husband, who happened to be watching Alex's livestream and I said "So when are we joining the party?" I joined soon afterwards. I made sure to tell the party that I'd been a Satanist beforehand as I did not want my murky past to embarrass your party in any way.

Your party, one which I thought had merit and decided join is the CPGB-ML, or the Communist Party of Great Britain (Marxist-Leninist) which is a party that I respect, despite the fact other so called communist groups in the UK don't like us much. Though most of these parties tell their followers to vote Labour, which doesn't seem a very communist stance to me.

So having joined up I got involved and came to lectures and seminars held by Joti Brar and the other party leaders, I love the Monday Marxism study class our party runs, and I attend most weeks. I feel our party is the only one in the UK actually doing proper communist work.

On the January morning at the pro Palestine march, I was approached by two policemen, one who asked me politely "Have you been speaking to a man with a beard wearing a black bomber jacket? This man is a terrorist and if you've been speaking to him you might be implicated too."

I said "I don't know, I've seen a lot of people today."

"We've been told he was talking to a woman in a red bowler hat, that's quite distinct, wouldn't you say?"

I couldn't think who they might have been on about so I went back to leafleting, having avoided giving them my details.

The rest of the march proceeded past with little incident, in defiance of MP Suella Braverman I waved a large Palestinian flag. As the end of the march came, I noticed a lot of policemen around, about fifty of them, and two riot vans and I thought, they are here for us.

I was told to step to one side by same policemen from before. I was told "This is going to sound dramatic but we are arresting you under section twelve of the terrorist act."

"What for passing out a leaflet?" I asked.

"It's the content of the leaflet, it is showing support for a terrorist organisation." one of the policemen said.

I stood silently beside them taking deep breaths, it was very cold and I was shaking nervously. A comrade came up to me and started to rub warmth into my arms, and then the police made him step to the side as well.

A person in a high viz orange jacket gave me a card with numbers for solicitors on it, I was anxious and didn't know if he was a comrade or not, so I put the card in my pocket and watched as the policemen raided our stall confiscating our leaflets. Then I was drawn to one side and checked over for weapons by a female police officer, before I was put in the waiting riot van. I had only just got the time to put my seatbelt on when the a policewoman said "Can you get in the back." pointing to the cage at the back of the van "Don't worry it isn't far."

About forty five minutes later we arrived outside Hammersmith police station and me and another comrade were unloaded, they had taken three of us off of the streets, fortunately my husband had been out of the way at the time.

They brought me into the cold foyer, telling me "Don't worry it's warmer inside." I was searched again for any drugs or suicide risk items.

Then I was brought into the police station and processed. First I was told about the cameras "They can see and hear everything that goes on in the station." then they asked me a manner of questions such as my general details and whether I had any medical conditions, if I'd been arrested before, have I ever attempted suicide? I told them, "Once while I was ill with schizophrenia but never since." I was asked do I need a duty solicitor? I said "No the party has one for me." and I handed them the card I'd been given earlier thinking it might contain the right number. All my affects were taken from me.

After the questions I was taken to be photographed and my DNA taken, then fingerprints were taken on a machine that does the process digitally. Then afterwards I was led to a cell, cell number ten, where I was to end up for the next twenty eight hours.

I took stock of my situation. I was in a cream walled cell, with a thick metal door, a painted blue stripe ran along the wall dividing it into two, there was a platform with a wipeable mattress that was to serve as a bed, a metal toilet, a domed silver mirror that looked like a staring eye, and a camera in the room and a bright bank of lights on the ceiling opposite the bed. I noted that this was no way to treat someone whose condition makes them believe they are being spied on.

A policewoman gave me a blanket through the hatch, but it was so warm in there anyway I didn't think I'd need it. I was given food and drink, I asked for water and a beef chilli from the selection I was offered. Then all there was to do, was to wait, I was initially supposed to be detained for twenty four hours but they extended it by another four.

There was very little to do, I'd been given a book by a mental health nurse who'd come to assess my condition, I'd picked A Clockwork Orange, it being one of the more compelling books on offer, but it was hard to focus on it given the situation.

Every twenty minutes the hatch would open and they would check on me, not that they really needed to disturb me, since there was a camera in the room. It took me till after seven at night, to get a phone call through to my husband, which gave me the impression that the police, like the NHS, are overstretched.

They told me when I got my phone call that I could tell my husband where I was but not the 'crime' for which I'd been arrested. It was a relief to speak with him, however briefly. I told him where I had been taken and he asked if I was okay. I said I was and that I'd had some food. The situation felt extremely surreal I'd never been in a cell before and I wondered how it was going to turn out, a small part of me thought "Well at least my life isn't boring."

From the intercom on my cell wall, the police buzzed in and asked me if I wanted my medication collecting from my house, I said no as one night without it wouldn't matter, however I knew this meant they'd be raiding my home, to look for whatever evidence they felt they needed to make a case against me.

I couldn't sleep at all during the night, the cells bright bank of lights were never switched off or turned down, and with people checking through the hatch every twenty minutes it was hard to get any sleep.

The next day I asked if I could brush my teeth and was eventually let out of the cell, attended, to be able to do so. I was given toothpaste and a short rubber toothbrush device, which in hindsight was supposed to be put over my finger, with my finger acting as the handle, I did not know this and had great difficulty brushing my teeth, the police officer attending me didn't bother to say how this toothbrush worked, and I didn't feel totally clean afterwards.

Back in my cell there was nothing to do but wait around, the window to the cell was a thick frosted glass, so greyed out that it was hard to tell if it was day or night outside, obviously designed so escape could not be planned.

I had an interview at about two in the afternoon with my solicitor present, and a person titled a responsible adult, because I had a mental health condition.

The interview was long and I was almost glad my solicitor had told me to answer no comment to everything, as it made the process quicker. The interviewers tried to trip me up with their questions by repeating ones they'd already asked, and the whole interview felt unfriendly.

Afterwards I was led back to my cell to wait the rest of my time out. It was before this interview that I was told my time would be extended. Originally they wanted to extend it by twelve hours, but said they could only manage six, my solicitor managed to get it reduced to four. I started crying when I realised my ordeal would not yet be over.

Realising I would not be released for another four hours I tried to get word to my husband to let him know. I did not realise and was not told that my husband and my comrades had been protesting outside the station all Sunday morning, or that another comrade Dr Ranjeet Brar had been grabbed off of the street outside the police station while my comrades protested.

It was only after I was bailed, with conditions, that I was told my husband knew I'd be let out at nine in the evening. The conditions of my bail were that I can not leave the country, that I can not be seen at a protest whether I planned to be there or not, and I cannot enter the London borough of Westminster.

I was led out of the station and given back my affects from the evidence bags, I was asked "Are you satisfied that the bags are empty?" I said "Yes." but when I put my satchel back on it was incredibly light, I took this to be because the police still had my phone. I was unceremoniously turfed out into the foyer, my husband and comrades were there and they applauded me and hugged me. As we waited for our other comrades to be released, I looked inside the satchel and saw my purse was missing, which had contained my bank card, my money, my train tickets, my two together rail card, my prepayment prescription card and my store cards.

I buzzed and asked for my purse to be returned to me, the

woman who had given me back my affects came out and said the whole purse had been taken as evidence, it had been taken as one item. Though I knew this wasn't right because in my satchel was my autism alert card, which had originally been in my purse.

I was upset but too tired to do much about it, I was annoyed at the prospect that if my comrades and husband had not been there to pick me up, I would have been kicked out of the station with no money no card, no phone, and no means of getting myself home, and a mental health condition.

Since I couldn't leave London that evening, I was given a lift to Ranjeet's Brar's house, he was still in detainment having been taken off of the street the day afterwards. But Ella his step mother let us in, she'd been protesting with everyone that day, and gave me and my husband a bed to sleep in. The party also paid for new train tickets to get us home the next day.

I didn't sleep much that night either. In total from getting up at six AM to be at the protest on the Saturday, I slept six hours out of sixty. It was early Monday that I got home, and I had to be at work later that day.

The experience was horrible, but I'm happy to note that you, the party, had my back, and despite what has happened I'm still happy to be a member. Once we'd sorted my mix up with the solicitor, the party sorted out legal representation for me and the others, we had meetings to try prevent such an occurrence happening again.

I found out at that meeting, that some people who had photographed me earlier on the Saturday, who I took as social history photographers, were from a state run, pro Zionist twitter blog called Harry's Place, they had put our images on twitter and tagged the Met Police, telling them to arrest us, and had even provided a map to our stall. It was all of those they photographed that ended up been taken from the street.

Though I had this terrible experience, which at the time of writing still hasn't yet been resolved, the police are still collecting evidence, though what they still need to collect I don't know. I'm really enjoying being with the party, I'm learning new things and hopefully growing as a person. One thing that I feel being in the party has helped with, is moving on, I have improved with my mental health far more than I ever realised I could. My current mental health nurse who I saw a few days after the ordeal, knew I'd been arrested as the police had contacted the crisis team, after I explained what went on to her, she gave me a clean bill of mental health and said I seemed the best she'd ever seen me.

Having tasks to do with the party, has helped me get past the illness, I've got different things to focus on other than my illness, and though I still mention it to people I do not feel it invading my life any more. I have gotten used to meeting new people, because there are a lot of comrades to meet with, I'm getting better at expressing my opinions and talking with people, even though there is still a way to go.

So I guess it's onwards and upwards comrades.

A Letter to Lucifer: Part 2
Doncaster
2023-present

Bye Bye my Old Friend

I cannot bear to speak to your picture,
about the changes I've been going through,
everything is feeling new,
and the ritual of saying goodbye makes me cry.
I held off as long as I could,
and I know you already know this,
I don't need to prove, that saying goodbye is hard.
As I sit here crying, trying to write these words,
I feel the end of an era coming,
and as usual I feel like running back to what I knew.
But I must go on,
I have to accept I am changing my life,
and my world is not ending,
but there is an ending in new beginnings.
I'll still see you as part of my life,
one that gave me direction, and kept me from strife.
And yes I still have belief,
but I cannot consider that belief as part of your name,
we must part ways,
and perhaps we'll meet again, at the end of days.

I loved you.

It was really this that motivated many of my behaviours whilst ill. For some reason my illness gave me a fetish for demons and for dark scenarios. The love I had for you was not the same love

I have for my husband. My husband and I have a mutual love, a slow burning love that hopefully will last many years to come.

The love I had for you was obsessional, primal. I never really knew why or where it came from. It was easy to love you in a way, when most of what I knew of you was created in my head.

I was never comfortable with the idea of fantasising about those I knew, because I realised in the cold light of day you have to look these people in the eye. So creating my own desires seemed a way around this. This way I could divorce myself from human connections.

But all things must end.

As I became more aware of myself post-illness I felt the Satanism became a bit embarrassing to me. While I was ill I had a certain lack of awareness, like a shield or force field. I was aware of things but my experience of the world was blunted, this made me feel more confident when acting the part of the evil Satanist. Yet as I became more well I was more aware of my Satanic shortcomings. I couldn't convince myself I was actually evil, so I'd talk to you and try to justify my religion to myself. I tried hard to reconcile with the fact that I'm not evil yet I worshipped a dark god.

After having taken the medication a lot of my adrenaline and excitement towards my religion started to fade, I wonder if my clinging to it for so long was because I was having difficulty moving on.

Over the years I started wearing my inverted cross less and less, because I felt more aware of the inflammatory nature of the symbol, for example I'd hide it from my violin teacher and others who I knew wouldn't approve.

As I started becoming more politically aware, I began realising even the shortcomings of LaVey's literature on Satanism, which has more politics in it than I first realised. So not only did I deviate spiritually from LaVey but also started to politically as well.

Satanism says a lot about thriving under the current system and doesn't advocate changing things for the better, as I became a communist, this didn't sit well with me especially as communism is about changing the current state of things.

Shedding my religion was not an easy decision for me, because it was something I'd defined myself by for so long. The process of my departure from Satanism was like a rollercoaster, not up and down, but a slow climb to the zenith before rushing down the other side.

I'd just finished what I thought was the last draft of this book in 2022 and it was written from a Satanic perspective, by September 2023 however, I'd joined the communist movement. For quite a while before I decided to become a communist, I'd find myself at work mulling over whether my religion could be carried alongside new found desire to be a communist. It's as if I could feel the world shifting beneath me, I wanted to change.

I decided in the end I'd have to let my religion go, or at least the notion of my beliefs being labelled Satanism, you could say it's the first real sacrifice I ever made. I made this decision alone, I didn't shed it because of the myth that communists hate religion, but because I felt the values Satanism holds are very capitalist. And if you are real in any capacity, you'd uphold the worst notions of imperialism and inequality.

Your picture, that I eventually framed, resides near my shrine not moved and ignored for months, I've still not been able to bear dismantling my shrine, losing my religion was not easy and made me feel strangely guilty.

I recently about June 2023 tried to reconcile with what I believed and I started a new book of shadows, partly to see if I could mend my belief system as I was a mass of contradictions, but I ultimately decided I couldn't and then later than that I joined the party.

So me and my husband went on this journey together. Though a person can have a religion and be a communist, religion is supposed to go on the back burner, so it doesn't conflict with party work.

It was much better for me to shed it. Even the symbol of you doesn't fit, so now I'm untethered religiously, but I have found something I always wanted, a sense of community, with a brilliant group of people who have my back and look out for one another.

So I guess this is goodbye, I'm moving on now and feel I need you less and less. So long and thanks for all the madness.

A Letter to Rob
Doncaster
2012-Present

The World

You Shattered my world,
But you are not my whole world now.
I have a new world to conquer,
more than you can offer.

I turned away from listening to you,
and am better for it.
You are but a buzz in my ear,
a silent nameless fear.

I need not your voices,
That completely vexed me.
Now I have grown,
and I don't have to conquer you on my own.

I met you in June 2012, at a gig I'd never intended to go to. My sister Rosie's then boyfriend— now her husband—was having a celebration for the first year of his radio show, and he'd brought together a bunch of bands to play. I hadn't planned on going to the gig because of it being in a pub, as at the time I wasn't keen on the noise and crowds in pubs.

Around this time, I still had difficulties going out alone. The illness had scarred me badly; I was afraid of people and of the hallucinations, and felt very vulnerable. But my sister insisted that I come along and suggested that my mum drop me round at her house so she could escort me to the gig. I'll admit I wasn't looking for love. I was still recovering from the serious symptoms of my illness, and I had very little interest in finding a partner.

I was on a newer antipsychotic medication called Aripiprazole which, while less effective at stabilising the symptoms, does have fewer side effects. I'd recently increased my dose of this medication to 20mg. My mum's theory is that it was the increased dosage that led me to my interest in you, since throughout the illness, and even leading up to it, I'd had no interest in going out with anyone. Though I would say that correlation does not always equal causation.

My own theory is that I was experimenting to see what might happen. As you know, I have a curious nature, and I often try things out to see what result I'll get. In this case I didn't expect that I'd fall in love, but this is exactly what happened.

When I first got talking to you, after the bands had finished playing, I was just seeing what reaction I might get. Though I hadn't failed to notice you looked handsome and looked like a kind person. We awkwardly discussed the clothes I was wearing that night and you suggested I looked like a time travelling assassin.

Even though I was just testing things out, I realised I was behaving foolishly. "Watch out, this could be the man you marry," I warned myself. I didn't think much of this thought though, and we went back downstairs to the bar area with my friend Amy. Back at a table, I started discussing the tea party I had planned for the next day, when Amy exclaimed loudly, "Since you're discussing it, maybe Rob would like to come to your tea party." I turned back to you and pointedly said, "Rob, would you like to come to my tea party?" You told me that you were due back in Aberystwyth the next day for uni, but that you had an open ticket, and could put off your return until the day afterwards.

So you ended up coming to my party. During the tea party, we were all talking and sharing stories, and I told you that I was asexual. I know that this caused you some confusion in working out whether or not I was interested in you.

After the party I made an effort to pursue you. I'd invite you to events whenever you were back from university, and on October the 23rd I asked you out after I'd cooked you a home-made chilli. When I say I asked you out, you'll remember that it was more like I awkwardly grabbed your hand and tried to explain why I liked you.

I'd noticed you had some interest in me romantically before I'd asked you out, which is what made me decide to act. It was the increase of touch that alerted me to the fact something romantic might be there between us. You would sometimes playfully run your hand across mine and lean close to me at times when we were out socialising. I'd not fallen in love at the time I asked you out but wanted to see where a relationship might take us. So when you playfully made a spider shape with you hand and ran it across mine on that night, I grabbed your hand and said, "I want to hold your hand."

You came to the Goth fest with me at Halloween and looked after me when I got slightly ill and paranoid while we were there. Fortunately, at the tea party I had told you about my illness. I confess that about two weeks in I got cold feet, and I felt like running from the relationship. But me being your first girlfriend gave me pause. I didn't want to run and leave you with a bad, and short, first relationship. So I stuck it out and saw my experiment through.

Telling me you'd had no prior relationships while at my tea party made me feel more inclined to pursue you. I felt inexperienced at relationships and knowing you had little experience as well, I figured I would feel safer around you, thinking we could learn together.

Two months in, I'd fallen in love with you. It hit me suddenly, like a sledgehammer, while we were talking. After that moment I felt that nothing else mattered. Every bad thing I'd been through didn't feel so bad: the voices, the bullying I'd suffered at university and school, the guilt I felt at the things I thought I'd done, all were wiped away.

I knew the feeling was a chemical one brought about by my hormones, and worried when my friend Emma told me that the chemical feeling of love wears off in eighteen months to two years, which is why couples often split up after that point.

This idea alarmed me because I didn't want to fall out of love with you. I worried that if my love for you was mere chemicals could it be over in two short years? I was genuinely afraid that with my egotistical nature I might start looking elsewhere. However, I never strayed. The love I have for you endured after the initial chemical high wore off.

In December 2012 you landed a job at the British Library as an archivist, and I was devastated that you'd have to leave, wondering what this might mean for us. The next phase of our relationship began, and I would commute to London once a month to see you, and you once a month back to Doncaster. We saw each other twice a month for brief weekends. This was to be our relationship for the next three years.

Going to London on the train was a massive step for me. I think it helped that I was so in love with you. I was always at the station about an hour early, for fear I'd miss the train announcements. I didn't want any unintended shocks. The first time I was going to go and see you it started snowing, and I was worried I wouldn't be able to make it. Fortunately, I managed to get an earlier train and missed the heavy snowfall.

We had some brilliant times in London. You would always be waiting for me by the barriers when I got off the train at King's Cross, and you'd look after me while I was there. You held my poor sense of direction in mind and kept me close by.

We'd go and see the sights and the shows and cook together at your shared house. We even took a trip on the Waverley paddle steamer, your favourite childhood ship, along the Thames to Southend. I was glad you chose to share these experiences with me.

It was the simple things we did that I remember best. We went walking in Greenwich Park in the snow and saw the squirrels fighting in the trees. We went to see the tall ships when the festival was on. We bought ice cream in Covent Garden and sat on a statue plinth to eat it, while looking at the adverts for musicals on the billboards. We didn't need to spend loads of money to enjoy ourselves; we'd sometimes take a backpack to the woods or a park and have a picnic there, just enjoying talking to one another.

We loved going to walk in Greenwich Park, and we went there often. I recall once when you called on the phone from London and told me that day you'd been to see the world's fastest tea clipper. I didn't understand the appeal at the time, partly because I didn't realise you were referring to a ship. I assumed you were referring to something which cut the leaves from the plant.

When I first saw the Cutty Sark in Greenwich, though, I was enamoured with it, and we went round the ship together. After that we would often sit near the Cutty Sark for a rest when visiting Greenwich. Our visits to Greenwich felt romantic, a feeling I would have scorned in the past.

The first musical we saw together was Wicked, and I remember how shocked you were at the price of the tickets. You had never seen a West End musical before, and you didn't realise how magical it was going to be. We saw it in February for my birthday and it was a freezing day. The dress I chose to wear was a little too thin for the weather, and you, realising I was cold, offered me your jacket. I insisted you keep it, though. Because of the side effects of my medication, I have a tendency to get very warm any time I start walking anywhere, which is a nightmare in summer. I knew you tended to take longer to warm up than I did, so let you keep the jacket (I figured it was my own stupid fault anyway for picking the dress, which was made of a thin damask). You enjoyed the experience of seeing the musical, and we have since seen many other musicals together. Seeing shows is still my favourite thing to do.

Your Doncaster visits were more relaxing. We'd stay at your parents' house because they had more room and share films and cook together and see relatives and friends. I'd always be waiting at your parents' house for you to come home, super anxious that your train might be delayed, but also excited to see you.

Over time it became harder and harder to leave each other behind at the end of the weekends, so we started thinking seriously about moving in together.

There was a time when you were leaving Doncaster to go back home; I was at the station with you, and we were waiting for your train. I was so in love that I yearned for you to say, "Come with me." I felt I wanted to run away with you and not have to stay in Doncaster alone. I knew my wish was futile. You were a lot more reserved about our relationship at the time, and tended to slow my pace down, which in hindsight was a good thing.

It was about four months into our relationship that I asked if I could come and live in London with you. This of course did not happen. Looking back, I think my state of being so in love was causing me to rush things. I'm glad we didn't move in together at that point, because you were still getting used to being in a relationship with me, and it would have been too much too fast.

Something you got me into, and that I never expected I would enjoy, is playing board games. The only games I had known like this before we met were children's board games such as Frustration or Cluedo, and of course Monopoly, which is a game I never really enjoyed. The first game we played together was Pandemic, which—as you told me—is a cooperative board game in which the players work together to defeat diseases. This piqued my interest, and the game, when we played with friends, was so intense and nerve-wracking that it remains one of my favourite board games. The rules to these sorts of board games are more complicated than an average roll the dice, move your pawn game, but are the better for it, and have some great themes.

Another thing you got me interested in was politics. Politics had always been a weak spot of mine. When I was younger I never knew anything about politics despite my boundless curiosity. I had always been interested in nature and the cosmos and the human psyche but had never gotten engaged with politics before. Al and his friends used to discuss politics, but I always felt somewhat out of my depth, not knowing where to even start with learning about it.

I didn't relate to politics in the same way I never had time for celebrity gossip, but I'm glad you've managed to get me engaged with it. Most of all you've helped sharpen my critical thinking tools. In the past I used to believe what the press told me, and not think about it too much. I'm now able, through a deeper understanding of things, to think critically.

You also got me more engaged with history, another weak area. You got me involved with a medieval re-enactment group which you were a part of. I confess to struggling with re-enactment a bit, despite enjoying learning about Norman history and getting to dress up and fight with swords. My struggles were that I was not good at making friends and I'd often spend a lot of time by myself during the day. Also, when camping, I had trouble sleeping, and re-enactment days start early.

Then there was all the kit we had to bring, which was heavy and unwieldy. I did enjoy some aspects of it, though. I learned how to five-finger braid and to use a lucet to make cord, and I also used some of my sewing skills. It was a lot of fun on occasions, and we got to camp in castles and on castle grounds.

I first got into your medieval re-enactment group when you were doing a show in Skipton. I had come to observe and got talking to one of the re-enactors about the possibility of joining. She told me she had some kit I could use, and I went from observing that day to being in the show.

A year and a half into our relationship I shocked you horribly by telling you about my religion. Because you were so shocked at my revelation I found it difficult to explain to you, and I didn't do a good job of alleviating your fears. On the weekend I told you about it, I had been complaining about suffering the effects of schizophrenia, so I think at first you thought I'd said this because I was ill.

At the time, after I'd told you about my religious affiliation, I was worried I'd wrecked our relationship. It felt to me as if I'd broken something innocent. But I felt I had to tell you because I was starting to think about writing a book about my experiences, and the Satanism can't really be separated from my schizophrenia. I'd wanted to be honest with you for a long time but couldn't really figure out the right time to tell you. Had I told you before we were in love, you might have walked away.

Over time my confession must have left your mind, and I

realised you had forgotten the incident. It was only very much later in our relationship, when we were living together, that I told you again. This was after I had purchased a book on Satanism which I thought might arrive at the weekend, causing you to wonder what I had ordered. At the time we were taking a trip to London together to meet up with one of your brothers who also lived there, and so I saw my chance to re-explain.

Often when I wanted to explain parts of myself to you that I feared you might find odd, I always told you when we were around other people. I would address my confession to whomever we were with, rather than tell you directly. This reduced my fear of the revelation. So it was that I mentioned to your brother while we were sat eating together that I had been very religious while ill, and that the religion had been Satanism. I didn't mention to him that I was still into it at the time, but it gave me an opening to discuss the subject with you again.

"Oh, I remember you mentioned that in my room in Walthamstow." you said.

I could tell you wanted to discuss it then and there, but I said, "Later."

It was in the park, after meeting your brother, that I had the chance to explain properly what Satanism was to me. I knew this time the confession would stick, and you'd remember it. It felt a great relief when you told me "It's up to you to explore anything you want, I can't stop you."

It took some time for my revelation to sink in, you even used to joke about me being evil, but at least now I've moved on. I did regret not telling you sooner, but I'm glad you accepted me around this time.

I didn't want to lose you because you give me so much. You keep me safe and secure and make me smile, and you've taught me many things.

At first when we started making real plans to live together, we thought we'd live in London, but the expense was a problem. Eventually you got a promotion at British Library, and you would be earning more money, so I tentatively suggested that we live back in Doncaster and you commute daily to London. At this point you'd been living in Chingford, and it took you an hour and a half to get to central London anyway. The journey from Doncaster to King's Cross, where the British Library is located, was only one hour and forty minutes.

To be honest, the prospect of living in London scared me, and I felt like a coward for suggesting we live in Doncaster. But it worked out well in the end. We eventually moved in together, into a two-bedroom house near Doncaster town centre. Before we combined our collective belongings, I thinned out my occult books and some of my scarier props. I kept my LaVey books and some gothic clothes and canes. I still have my picture of Lucifer, but gone is the scary doll I made, and some of my other weird props. I feared coming across as too strange. Even though we'd been together for three years by then, I was still worried I might scare you off. I do regret that I got rid of many of my occult things as they were part of my past, but after all they are only things, and you are far more important to me.

Living together was something I fretted about. We were going from a relationship where we'd seen each other on weekends to one where we would see each other constantly. I was worried that something might change between us, that we might go off one another when our annoying habits were out in the open. There was also the open question of whether we would be able to fill time with conversation or would we simply run out of things to say. But my fears were unfounded.

We managed to not fight too much and to tolerate our differences, and we also never seemed to run out of things to talk about, even though we spent most of our time together. I also found I was content when I was in the house alone while you were at work. I managed to find things to do, like artwork or cleaning, or going to the market. There was something delightfully normal about living a life away from my mum's house and sharing a home with you. It didn't seem odd at all.

My mental health has improved a lot since meeting you. You take the time to keep me social, and we have gotten up to many things together. I am no longer always scared to leave the house, and you try your best to find ways to keep me distracted from the voices I still hear. We have managed to get through all of the trials life has thrown at us so far.

After six years of us being together, you took me to York and proposed to me next to the Mallard steam engine at The National Railway Museum. I'd been hoping you'd propose for quite some time and delightedly said yes. You even landed a job at Doncaster archives before we were due to be married, which meant you'd be around while I was planning the wedding.

I surprised myself by managing to plan our wedding. After I booked the venue and the registrar, I became worried about the fact that we were now going to have to find the money to pay for it all, since the date was set and everything was official. But I rose to the challenge. The dress I wanted was on the pricey side, but I sold art and even helped with painting up an old lady's house to raise the money. While you worked I'd plan, keeping the structure of the wedding simple and fairly traditional. I ended up making a lot of the wedding decorations and favours myself. I created my own table plan and used a pyrography machine to make place names. I even designed the invitations and save the date cards.

We ended up having a lovely wedding in the ballroom of Doncaster mansion house. Of course, in my typical fashion I didn't choose a white dress, but one with black lace over red silk, making it look burgundy. The lace was embroidered in silk with poppies and green leaves. Poppies are an important flower to me because I used to draw them when I was deeply ill.

I couldn't have asked for a more perfect day, but of course it is you that matters most to me. I am very much still in love with you. Love is a wonder I had never felt before. You are the best possible outcome of any experiment, and I hope you continue to keep me safe and warm.

Letter to the Voices: Part Thirteen
Doncaster
April-2007

Justice

"I'm not mad." I said.
"Come on please, just take the meds."
I took them eventually,
after much persuasion.
They were powerful and they wiped you out...
Well almost.

I no longer believe your lies,
and no longer wear a disguise.
I'm getting there day by day.
Slowly recovering and living my life.
Pain slips away and it feels nice,
however, I must say it's not justice.

After my mum had taken me to the doctor, I was sent for an assessment at the mental health unit round the side of the hospital. I didn't quite understand why, or where, I was being sent. My mum, who knew more about what was going on than me, was extremely concerned. She was worried I was going to be locked up.

I can't recall the face of the woman who conducted the interview, but it took place in a room with leather sofas and bookshelves. There was a large window at one end of the room. The woman asked my mum questions, and I could hear you mocking me from somewhere beyond the window.

The woman then turned to me. "Can you hear them inside or outside your head?" she asked.

"Outside, obviously." I told her in an insolent tone.

"Can you hear them now?"

"Yes."

"Do you intend to harm yourself?"

"No." I'd forgotten the incident at the fourth storey window, and would only recall it again once I'd got over the shock. I even insisted to my mental health team soon after the illness that I'd never been suicidal, unable at the time to recall that this had happened.

"Do you intend to harm other people?"

"No." I'd forgotten the fact that in my muddled state I'd nearly hurt someone.

The nurse sent me home but told my mum they'd be sending the crisis team to monitor me for four days.

In those last days your torture was so bad I spent most of my time laid on the floor of my mum's living room trying not to provoke you. I'd lie with my arm flung over my face to stop you seeing my facial expressions, but you'd just accuse me of pretending to be dramatic. To help me sleep, the doctors prescribed me some potent sleeping pills. They only supplied three days' worth because they were powerfully addictive.

I took one of these pills that evening, but I was so frightened I might never wake up that I asked my mum to come in and check I was still breathing. When she climbed up to my canopy bed to check on me, I woke up and lunged at her, growling. She almost fell down the steps. In the morning I found that the sleeping pills had given me some rest but made little difference to your presence. I wanted to escape your rumours and torments so badly that I—an unseasoned traveller with no money—

imagined running away to America, and seriously wondered if it would be possible.

In a fit of creativity, I produced a sketchbook full of drawings, pictures of me with words coming out of my head. The pictures were another way of contacting you, of letting you know what I was thinking and feeling. I still have this sketchbook because my mum saved it for me, even though I'd wanted to bin the relics of my past after I was first medicated.

After three days there was no change in my condition. I was in a black pit of despair, and the psychiatrist was called. He arrived at my grandma's house because that's where I was spending the day while my mum was at work. I was sitting on the sofa, and when the psychiatrist arrived, he sat in a chair some distance away from me. I was convinced he was offended by my smell, but now I think he sat further away to prevent danger if I were to get violent.

He asked me questions—what they were I can't remember—and eventually prescribed me a course of Olanzapine at a dose of 10mg. A nurse came to my mum's house later that night to explain the medication to me and convince me to take it. The mental health team had told my mum that they would come each night to deliver the pill, which I assume was to prevent me taking them all at once in a suicide attempt. The nurse told me the pill might make me gain weight, and that I'd probably feel tired on it. "I'll try them for two weeks." I said, "I'm not mad." I was completely unconvinced that they'd work.

No one had told us what the pills were treating, possibly because the doctors don't want people becoming alarmed and booting the sufferer out of the house. So my mum looked the pills up on the internet and realised they were for paranoid schizophrenia. She asked me downstairs to come look at the information on the screen. "No, they are trying to make me look mad." I said angrily, "I don't have schizophrenia."

After I had recovered, I wondered why mum had done this, since it was clear that I was ill and equally clear that I'd never believe the information she was showing me. I realise now she was testing me to see if I'd believe I was ill or not, to help confirm her suspicions. I could hear you jeering at me all the while and could feel my world unravelling all around me. I felt I was teetering on the brink, not realising I'd already been clinging to the edge for a long time.

That evening my mum tried to talk me into taking the tablet, a pill I didn't believe I needed. I was convinced that it would harm me if I took it because I clearly didn't have schizophrenia. Eventually I gave in and told her, "Okay. Give me the madness pill." I felt exasperated that no one believed I was telling the truth about you. I took the pill and went to bed, because it was late, and the medication had a sedating effect.

On waking the next morning, I felt odd. My mind was a lot quieter, and I could barely hear you. Suddenly I realised I didn't believe I was being spied on. I went downstairs and in a trembling voice said to my mum, "I don't believe I'm being spied on any more." Mum embraced me and we both cried.

It took quite a while for the entire delusion to melt away. For a long time, I believed that it was real bullying at university which had triggered the schizophrenia. For a long while I'd write in books trying to figure out what parts had been real and what parts hadn't. Eventually the entire delusion peeled away, and I realised that right from the start I'd been wholly under its influence.

A Letter from Me to You Dear Reader
Doncaster
April 2007- Present

The Sun

Recovery it's a journey,
not a straight line from points A to B.
But a long meandering road,
it leads back and forth, it's taking hold.

Through the woods and dark mountains,
past the city's ornamental fountains.
Very near the edge of a precipice,
whose mournful pull makes me step back a bit.

Travelling this never-ending journey.
Little by little, I climb out of that mire,
"Why can't the road be straight?" I enquire.
Why does the path feel ever so dire?

One step forward, one step back.
Two steps forward, one step back.
Three steps forward, one step back.

But of this journey I never can tire.
Moving steadily onwards and out of that fire.

In the immediate aftermath of my illness, I was very afraid. I didn't like people seeing my facial expressions and I wore sunglasses a lot. I would periodically decide I didn't want to be a goth because people might stare at me. So I would alternate through phases of not being gothic or being gothic depending on my wavering tolerance for being stared at.

I remember having an appointment with a psychiatrist called—appropriately—Dr Goodhead. I remember going into his office with my mum and him asking me if I would take my sunglasses off, because with them on I reminded him of a devil worshipper or a vampire. I am not sure why he said this but wonder now if he was testing me. My mum was terrified I might tell him I was a Satanist and be locked up as a result.

Obligingly, I removed my sunglasses.

The doctor asked me "What illness do you think you have?"

I answered slowly, "Paranoid schizophrenia."

He pushed my file across the desk and opened it. The words PARANOID SCHIZOPHRENIA were emblazoned across the front page.

This, the story of my schizophrenic experience, has been very hard to tell. It always pains me to remember the things I thought and did. But I've done my best to be as honest as I could within the limits of my memory. I had difficulty in piecing together some elements of my story because they were too complicated to explain, and others because of their sheer absurdity. So much of what happened in my flat, under the glow of my red light, remains hazy and indistinct.

There are some parts I haven't come to terms with. If I hadn't taken pleasure in some of the things the voices said, then my story may have been easier to tell. Fortunately, writing and remembering is cathartic as well as painful.

One question remained for me: whether I am a psychopath. I first asked this question after reading an article about psychopathy I happened to stumble upon. I read that one of the defining characteristics of the psychopath is a grandiose sense of self-worth. This stood out to me because I have always wondered why I loved myself so much when so many others pick fault with themselves. A few other characteristics, such as my conning behaviour, my lack of impulse control, being prone to boredom, and an appetite for experimentation, felt familiar.

I did broach this with one of my doctors, but he thought the picture didn't fit me. Indeed, there are characteristics of psychopathy I don't display. I certainly don't have the typically promiscuous behaviours associated with psychopathy, or the desire to take drugs.

I'd like to find out why I behaved in a psychopathic manner. I would like to understand why I behaved the way I did; why in the past I was deceptive, impulsive, charming, charismatic, and lacking in empathy. I also had a sense of entitlement, as if I deserved fame and power, and I've described at length in this book my tendency to play games.

I also wonder sometimes if the schizophrenia changed my personality, its symptoms mirroring narcissism. Perhaps the antipsychotic drugs I am taking might also dampen some of the aspects of psychopathy and narcissism. But this is sheer speculation. What is certain is that these days I am a much nicer person, and a better behaved one. I am not as haughty nor as entitled as I used to be, and I always try to resist my less pleasant impulses.

Recovering from schizophrenia is no laughing matter, and it wasn't easy. I was tired most of the time and wanted to die in my sleep. I was bored, and surprisingly lonely without the voices, and it took a lot to get to the place I am at now.

I'd lost weight whilst ill, around four stone, so I was also physically depleted.

Optimising my medication is an ongoing project. After a while on Olanzapine at 10mg—which made me feel like a zombie—I moved onto 15mg of Aripiprazole Then up to 20mg. The side effects of Aripiprazole are far less, but it doesn't get rid of the symptoms as well. I still occasionally get ill and sometimes have visual hallucinations. The voices are always with me, and I believe they always will be.

I have now managed to reduce my medication to 10mg.

I'm luckier than some people with schizophrenia. I have a good support network who watch out for me, and I have a high level of awareness of my condition so I can also watch out for myself. I'm in the fortunate percentage of people who could escape the illness: 25% of sufferers never recover, and 15% of sufferers never find a medication which works for them. Sadly 10% of people with schizophrenia die by suicide.

I've done okay in the aftermath of my illness. I'm currently in long-term work, I've had various minor art exhibitions based on my mental health, and have done talks on my illness. In 2013 I was shortlisted for an arts in health competition in Milton Keynes, where I got to exhibit a body of work. Rob helped me get to the exhibition on the train because I was nervous about travelling alone. I have sold my art, too. Some of my work featured in a play called The Black Stuff, a musical about Charles Goodyear, the inventor of vulcanised rubber. I was part of a collective of artists who ran their own gallery, but this has ended now. Nowadays I'm doing party work and enjoying studying with and meeting my comrades.

I still have a selection of long coats, though they are more normal looking than before, and some of them are even in colours other than black. I still have links to my gothic past. One of my favourite necklaces consists of lots of skulls carved from a deer antler.

I still don't feel fully comfortable being human, which is only to be expected, as real stories rarely have a clean resolution. But I am proud of what I've achieved. The greatest achievement of my recovery from schizophrenia was realising I'm capable of love.

Though I don't owe anyone my story, I think it is important to share it. We are made up of stories. We are the sum of our experiences, and I like to think that my story can help others understand this highly stigmatised illness. I want to give the gift of hope. Hope is all we really have: the hope that things might get better, and that after the darkness the sun might shine again.

Epilogue

I am not a bad person, even though I have sometimes pretended to be. Despite my darkness, there is also a lot of light in me. I have a profound sense of wonder and boundless curiosity, I'm imaginative and creative, and I have trouble destroying things I perceive to be beautiful or well made. I am diplomatic and polite, I like singing, and my pet cats delight me. I enjoy beautiful places and art. I believe I am intelligent and highly self-actualised, even though I have in the past used these attributes to treat people badly.

Much of my story shows me through the lens of my illness, and I fear that to some it could seem that I deserved what happened to me. But I did not deserve it, and my illness was so painful that I would never wish it upon anyone. I read once in an article that the stress of suffering with schizophrenia is more intense than the stress experienced by a soldier on a battlefield. With schizophrenia the stress doesn't end, and persists for months rather than for a short swathe of time.

Schizophrenia took away my chance to find myself, to learn to live away from home, and to stand on my own two feet. This illness is a thief. It not only took away everything that mattered to me, but it also robbed me of my sanity and my ability to live the kind of normal, carefree life so many people take for granted. While I live, I must consider how everything will impact my mental health. There is a long list of things I can't do because I have to babysit my sanity, or because I have fears surrounding my illness.

My reality is not the reality of other people. I must constantly check in with the people around me to help me decide what is real and what isn't. I contend with visual, auditory, and olfactory hallucinations, as well as the negative symptoms of schizophrenia I have mentioned before. I live with the ever-present fear that comes with not knowing the answers to basic existential questions. What is reality? Who am I? Which of my senses can I trust?

Schizophrenia can shorten the lifespan by about ten to twenty years. It's not certain whether this is due to the unhealthy lifestyles some sufferers have, or the medication, or even the structure of the brain due to the illness. Scientists aren't entirely sure why.

There are so many unanswered questions. That's why I know I must always try and find meaning, in my illness, in my life, and in the universe. And though I'll miss those times when I felt the whole world was all about me, I've been able to move on from my illness by realising the world doesn't revolve around me… and nor should it.

The End

Now onwards to the next chapter.

About the Author

Helen Astin-Hardman

Helen, born in Doncaster, pursued her studies in Fine Art at Huddersfield University, where she faced the challenge of being diagnosed with paranoid schizophrenia. Much of her artwork and writing is inspired by this experience. A lifelong learner at heart, Helen's hobbies are as diverse as they are creative. She enjoys singing, creating art, playing the violin, embroidery, and immersing herself in Dungeons & Dragons. Writing has become another avenue of expression for her.

This memoir marks Helen's first venture into publishing—a deeply personal reflection on her life and mental health journey. She is a passionate advocate for mental health awareness and hopes that sharing her story will encourage others to open up about their own experiences.

Helen currently lives in Doncaster with her husband and their beloved cat, Wolfie.

Connect with Helen:

Email: helenhardmanart@hotmail.co.uk

Instagram: @helenhardmanart

thehellhereproject.co.uk